SET
FREE

SET FREE

An Hachette UK Company
www.hachette.co.uk

Summersdale Publishers Ltd
Part of Octopus Publishing Group Limited
Carmelite House
50 Victoria Embankment
LONDON
EC4Y 0DZ
UK

www.summersdale.com

Printed and bound by CPI Group (UK) Ltd, Croydon, CR0 4YY

ISBN: 978-1-84953-960-9

Substantial discounts on bulk quantities of Summersdale books are available to corporations, professional associations and other organisations. For details contact general enquiries: telephone: +44 (0) 1243 771107 or email: enquiries@summersdale.com.

SET FREE

A LIFE-CHANGING JOURNEY FROM BANKING TO BUDDHISM IN BHUTAN

EMMA SLADE

summersdale

SET FREE

A LIFE-CHANGING
JOURNEY FROM BANKING
TO BUDDHISM IN BHUTAN

EMMA SLADE

In honour of friendship

CONTENTS

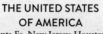

THE UNITED STATES OF AMERICA
Santa Fe, New Jersey, Houston,

THE UNITED KINGDOM
Whitstable, Cambridge, Kilve, Faversham

HAWAII
Maui

COSTA RICA
San José

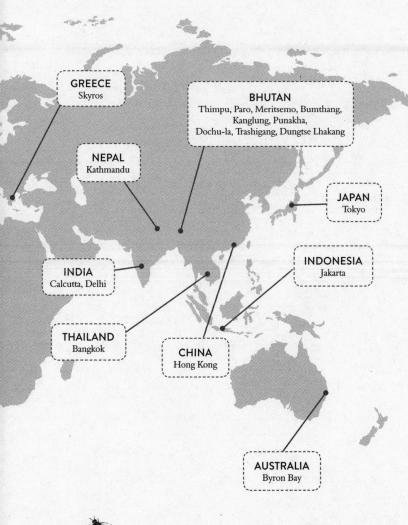

GREECE
Skyros

BHUTAN
Thimpu, Paro, Meritsemo, Bumthang,
Kanglung, Punakha,
Dochu-la, Trashigang, Dungtse Lhakang

NEPAL
Kathmandu

JAPAN
Tokyo

INDIA
Calcutta, Delhi

INDONESIA
Jakarta

THAILAND
Bangkok

CHINA
Hong Kong

AUSTRALIA
Byron Bay

INVITATION

If you come with me now, I will show you the sky.

We will lie on our backs on a mountainside

and watch the white clouds come and go.

We will fill our minds with birdsong and

the gentle wash of a river far below.

If you come with me now, I will

show you how we got there.

PART 1

BUDDHA

CHAPTER 1
THE WIGGLE

I was feeling a little sexy. There was a wiggle in my walk. It was the shoes. I was wearing my black slingbacks bought with a lot of money and a dose of guilt. I had loitered outside the impeccably clean glass window of the shop on Sloane Street in London. Here a few choice shoes were arranged on slim-stemmed white stands. It was too much of a temptation. I went in and pounced: gotcha!

It was lovely to hear the *click clack* of these elegant heels now as I walked up the wide, polished stone stairs of the Grand Hyatt Hotel in Jakarta, Indonesia. I was in a five-star hotel and I was feeling pretty five-star myself. No supermodel, but tall in an expensive, fitted black suit with tightly upholstered buttons. The meeting I had come from had gone well. I was a woman in a man's world and I was doing fine, thank you very much. Not bad for a girl who had grown up in a quiet seaside town where you could taste the salt in the water and the smell of whelks hung in the air.

There was none of that here in the humid air of Asia. The leaves were large enough to let drops of afternoon rain settle on top of them, perfectly still. Now, on this warm evening in September 1997, I was setting out how the rest of my day would unfold. I would get to the room, change into my swimming costume and go to the beautiful, underlit hotel swimming pool. I had glimpsed it from above, all deep blue reflections edged by discreetly moving staff carrying single drinks on round trays. Then I would eat something light and sensible, appropriate for a corporate female, and meet up with Greg and anyone he had with him later on. There – everything was set. Now it was just a question of the follow-through.

I always liked checking out hotel rooms; the smooth bed covers and range of mini-toiletries. At this hotel, my room was on the fourth floor, a short walk down a blank corridor and on the right. I had no doubt the corridors on all the other floors were identical.

The room was large, bigger than the whole of my old flat in Hong Kong. Space was always at a premium in Hong Kong and my flat in Lan Kwai Fong was small and lined with mirrors to give the impression of spaciousness. It could be disconcerting after a few drinks. This hotel room was a world away: big enough to have both empty space and carefully placed objects, like pieces set out on a chessboard. It was so nice to have space, the feeling of freedom.

Inside and to the left was the bathroom door, followed by a cream wardrobe, then a sitting area with an antique-style dressing table and accompanying stand-up mirror. Opposite the entrance door there was a large glass window divided into squares by thick grey lines. In front of that stood a large desk with a rectangle of leather set into it and an ornate European-style wooden chair. It seemed the room might be ready for a grand visitor in the style of Napoleon himself. Further round to the right a bed was positioned with narrow spaces available on either side of it. Big – impressive, even – and all mine to spread out in like a lottery winner falling back in delight.

I put my laptop in its zipped black case on the desk by the phone. I took off my silver necklace and square-faced watch. I'd flown in on the early-morning flight from Hong Kong and it had been a long day. I pushed off my shoes and dropped by a couple of inches; I felt my feet sigh and my calf muscles relax. *Nice.*

Padding along in my tights, jacket off, shirt loosened, I went to check out the bathroom. Slowly I washed my hands with the just-opened mini-tablet of soap, smelling its scent before use. Looking around I saw there were only two towels. One close by, and small, and one far away folded on top of a chrome wall radiator. *Only two?* I checked under the counter but, yes, there were definitely only two.

Hmm. That's a bit rubbish for a five-star hotel. Would they have others at the pool, or was I supposed to use these for my swim and then survive on a little hand towel? *Hummph.*

Tricky.

Should I phone up housekeeping? Would I be a spoilt brat complaining about a 'lack' of towels in a room you could hold a ping-pong tournament in?

I checked my face in the mirror. My eyebrows were neat, my hair swept up from my neck, and the raspberry lipstick was still oozing out its colour, defining the arches of my lips. The lighting in the bathroom was flattering, a good backdrop for the appearance of a successful businesswoman. I enjoyed a mildly triumphant air guitar moment. I knew for certain that Dad would be proud of me. This is what he had wanted for his eldest child. He would have been proud of the suit, the shoes and the business trips. He would be telling his mates down the pub on a Sunday lunchtime. I could see him leaning on the bar, friendly and affable in his wellies, taking a break from digging potatoes in his weekend allotment.

He had said it, long ago: 'Em, I can see you in investment banking, you know.' He had been watering the garden from a large green watering can with a perforated copper spout, while I was trailing round the grass, noticing my newly large feet walking below me. The evening was one of warm air mixing into autumn and the soil was dry and crumbly. I must have been ten or eleven and had no idea what investment banking was except it sounded like something only men did. But I was pleased there was something Dad could see me 'doing'. It felt good to have something to share and hope for, together. Nice he was thinking of my future as he watered the plants.

Odd how these moments stay with you, never quite sinking back into the category of The Past.

'That's my daughter,' I could hear him say.

I put on my one-piece, turquoise swimming costume, my head elsewhere. It was the perfect colour for my English skin and dark blonde hair.

Still mulling over the question of towels and the feeling of Dad-ness, I heard a knock at the door. I slipped on the white hotel dressing gown and went to open it, not paying particular attention. Perhaps I was vaguely expecting towels, dry cleaning or a welcome gift.

Instead a gun was pushed straight at me.

Hard, silent metal into the soft centre of my chest. Bam.

I stumbled backwards into the room, my feet caught under me like a horse being put down.

What?

The man with the gun got me from behind, placed his hand over my mouth and pushed me down on to the carpet. I tried to cower to make my body curl smaller, instinctively covering my head with my empty hands. I shrank. The man stood over me with the gun.

Inside a room on the fourth floor of a five-star hotel, I started pleading for my life. The words came automatically, desperately.

'Oh God, please don't kill me.' My words clung to my teeth and my whole body was cold.

It was all changing so quickly. I knew he could hurt me at any time. From above, from the side, on my head, in my stomach, he could hit me or kick me and I did not know how to protect myself. All I had left were these words.

'Please. Please don't kill me.' *Beg.* 'Jesus. God. Please.' My mind was preparing for a bang or a hole or a thud.

I *never* said 'Jesus'; I rarely said 'God'. So why now? It was the only name I could implore to. If I had known this man's name, I might have used that instead.

Am I about to die?

I was in a towelling robe with a swimming costume on. I was English. I was female. I had a good job. I was a success. I had all this. I couldn't take it in.

For a few moments, I moved outside my body. My mind somehow jumped out. I was pleading to live and witnessing the end of my life, all at the same time. I felt so temporary.

But I didn't want to be. I wanted to live, and I knew it with absolute certainty.

I don't want to die.

When it came down to it, I was scared of dying. I had not realised this before – that I was so scared of what might happen next.

The man pushed me back into one of the spaces between the bed and the desk. Crouching, I could hear the sound of rough breathing in my throat. I was back in my body. I was still alive. Hearing this sound was like knowing that time was passing for me for the very first time. Inhale, and one second was gone; exhale, another second came and went.

Peeping up at the large, gridded window, I realised it was in fact sealed. The grid lines were just decorative – they weren't frames that could be opened. I knew then that even if I were to pick up my heavy laptop and launch it through the window, it would not let me escape. And anyway I was four floors up. I would smash to the ground by the bright blue pool.

The room was a square, escape-proof box and I was in it.

I was trapped by this hotel room, by the small space between the bed and the desk, and by this man and his gun. I knew that if I moved suddenly I would be shot. On my left, the bed was laid with a shiny satin bedspread. A pattern was stitched into its salmon-pink surface and its trimmed edge was hanging next to me. The fibres of the floor carpet were close to my face. With my head down, I could glimpse the man's shoes pacing backwards and forwards in front of my downturned eyes. When they came close, I froze; when they moved away, I sweated. My mind grasped at cop-show plots from TV shows and movies. *How do I survive?*

What do I do?

I thought that I would be safer if I didn't look at his face. Then, somehow, I would be able to convince him that I was no danger to him, that he could let me go.

So, with my head down, I listened.

The pointy tips of the man's shoes were far away and then close by, as if on a camera runner moving from telephoto to wide angle. There it was – that slight creak as the feet moved.

I became aware of a strange smell. Was that the smell of fear? Maybe it was just how his body smelt this evening. Rank in my nostrils.

Then he was over to my right side, near the desk. I could hear him picking at things, the chink of jewellery being turned over; he must be fingering my watch.

Bill had given me that watch. It was his first present to me, given to celebrate our 'officially' becoming an item. We bought it together on the ground floor of Harvey Nichols, close to my July birthday. It was the most expensive present I had ever been given; it had a square, silver perimeter and a round, blue stone set into the edge.

From above my head, I heard, 'You are Emma A. Slade?'

The man's voice was reading out my name, pronouncing it carefully. Hearing my name was like hearing it in a line-up for execution. Fear tightened inside me. He must have been looking through my handbag, slung on the chair, and found my bank card.

What can I possibly say to that? My throat clenched and my stomach felt empty – sick.

Why was he asking my name? Did he know me? Had he been sent to find me? Had I really created such a stir with my questions in the finance meetings today? If this situation was deliberate, specific to *me*, then it definitely did not bode well.

'You *are* Emma A. Slade?' he said once more. He wanted an answer. His voice was accented but its origin was not clear to me.

'Yes, yes,' I answered. It was true after all.

Suddenly, the telephone on the desk began to ring. It took us by surprise. I looked up, in search of instructions. The man I saw had a thin face. He wore a grey, slightly shiny suit. If I'd been standing up I would have been taller than him. He was Asian but, like his accent, I could not tell from exactly where. Despite the shiny shoes and the gun, he seemed nervous. This was unsettling. It was not reassuring to have a man with a gun being twitchy so close to you.

The telephone continued; it was so loud in the room.

I waited.

Are you going to pick it up?

It kept on ringing.

Should I pick it up?

The man signalled with the gun for me to move; it was going to be my job to stop the ringing. On my knees, shuffling sideways, I moved the small distance to the desk on my right side. He walked closer and stood by me, to my left. I crouched a little as I lifted my arm up to reach the phone on the desk.

I put it to my right ear.

'Hello?' It was *my* voice sounding shaky. That was me.

A man said, 'Hello. Sorry to disturb you but there have been reports, from the room next to you, of screaming. Is everything OK?' The voice was clearly anxious.

I heard all this in my ear but had no idea if the man standing next to me had also heard them.

I held my breath, saying nothing, waiting to see if the armed man did anything.

A pregnant pause.

He didn't grab the phone. He just did nothing. Was he waiting for something?

Underneath the silence, I realised that I could let someone know what was happening.

This is your chance. Say something.

But my throat was stuck. If I said 'Yes' and the man *had* heard, his metal gun would hit my head and my body would fall... I could see it now.

The man on the phone spoke again, insistent: 'Is there someone there with you?'

I spoke the three letters out loud to make one simple word: 'Yes.'

'Do you need help?' The response came fast through the phone. The man in the room was looking past me intently.

Gaining courage, I repeated, more evenly, 'Yes.'

'OK, we are coming.' The voice was definite.

I said, 'Thank you,' as if I had been offered a hot towel or a porcelain cup of tea.

'Right, goodbye then.' I guess there wasn't much else to talk about.

'Goodbye,' I said, just as you do when you are ending any conversation. The word you use when you leave someone behind.

I put the phone down on its cradle, slowly, as if this moment was time I could stretch out without end.

I waited for the man with the gun to react but he did not. Instead, preoccupied, he moved away.

He didn't ask me about the call. I wondered if his English actually wasn't that good. He hadn't answered my pleas and, so far, all he had said was, 'You are Emma A. Slade?'

Perhaps I had got away with it. Rescue was on its way. I held on to this secret like holding down a champagne cork before it blows.

Did I scream when I opened the door? I didn't remember screaming, but who cared now that they were coming?

In my head John Wayne appeared with horses and chaps and the swagger of a saviour. Things had changed a little, all behind the back of this shiny man.

I shuffled over to rest on the side wall of the bed, legs still bent, feet behind me. I didn't move right back into the little space I had been in before though.

The man became more twitchy, a little sweaty. It struck me that maybe he was on drugs. He was the villain after all. Fidgety, he paced the room, as if beginning to sense its limits.

I looked up a little more decisively.

He resumed walking back and forth towards me. As he did so, he kept fidgeting with his belt. His jacket was open and there was a pale, thin belt with a metal clasp threaded through his trousers. It looked cheap on his slim hips. This was a human on the prowl with a rope around its middle. I shuffled further back towards the wall and my hiding space and shrank a little smaller. There were no cowboys circling the perimeter. My body felt vulnerable. Even my bony backbone felt soft and snappable as I curled forwards to protect my front.

Besides the creak of his walking and the noise of my breathing the room was so quiet. I knew time was passing although there was no sound of a clock ticking. I felt much older.

No one else had arrived.

A new kind of fear took hold of me.

When the man on the phone said 'goodbye', what *had* he meant?

Trying not to feel – let alone show – my concern, I began to think that no one was coming after all. An unshareable panic began to run in my mind. Quickly it moved; worse and worse it became, one fear spawning another, until I felt suffocated.

Maybe the call was staged? Could it be a set-up, part of some weird plot? Maybe the man in the room had known the call was coming. Maybe he had deliberately not reacted?

England was so far away. My mum, the beach and the sunny garden – they were all very somewhere else. I realised that no one I loved knew where I was. This would mean that no one would know. If it ended. Here. Tonight.

There was just me and him and the gun. This gun with its rounded end looking at me; the 'me' that had just turned thirty-one. The 'me' that was single. The 'me' that so wanted to be happy and make a success of life.

But what had I done, really? I had no children. I hadn't managed to become happy with being me yet. I had messed it up, damn it. And now it was going to be too late – too late to make it better. *Damn it, Emma, you've fucked it up.* Wanting towels and hotels and thinking it would all be OK if you got a good job. It would be such a waste to have it end here, now. *Damn it.*

I looked again at the useless window and gave in to exhaustion.

Then there was a loud bang on the door. We both jumped, together. I looked up and we looked at each other. We looked properly for the first time.

What shall I do? I didn't say the words, but signed them with my eyebrows, with my face. *What do you want me to do? You tell me. You're the one with the gun.*

The man signalled, again with a loose flick of his gun. I had to get up and go towards the door. As I did so, he caught me from behind, placing the right of his body to my left side. Standing there, I felt the gun in my back. I could feel its round shape, pushing. I held on to my white robe to cover the front of me, the parts of me that felt so female.

As we walked forwards, as if miming a child's three-legged walk, I could see the hotel door had outstanding ridges set on to it like a complex picture frame. Then I saw there was one of those little peepholes with a hinged silver cover on it which you could flick up or flick down.

Why had I not seen it before? Why had I not used it? *Stupid, Emma. So stupid.*

Slowly, I opened the door. It moved towards me, swinging inwards to the left. It was solid, weighty; it felt good just to hold on to something.

He was behind me, further round to the left. I had no awareness of his hands, of whether they were touching me or not; the feeling of the gun was enough to restrain me.

I angled my head round the edge of the door, leaving most of my body in the room and inching my neck and head out. It wouldn't be possible for anyone to see the man behind me. He was safe.

Out in the corridor was a hotel man in a suit, poised like a butler. He looked at me and asked, 'Is everything OK, madam?'

I just looked and said, 'Yes'.

I nodded.

What else can I say? I hoped my expression, the nodding like a puppet and my lockjaw expression would scream out to him that *OF COURSE I AM NOT OK. THERE IS A MAN WITH A GUN IN MY BACK AND I CANNOT GET OUT OF THIS ROOM.*

But I didn't know how to do that. I had no idea how to extend the conversation from there, how to play for time.

I said, 'Thank you' with an attempt at a quizzical tone.

He returned it, plain-faced. 'Thank you, ma'am. Goodbye.'

Hearing another 'goodbye' was like a thud – so damning, so final. Everything turned inwards once more and I knew I could not say that word again myself. Instead my head made one slow nod – like a puppet taking a bow at the end of a play.

I closed the door.

There was nothing else I could do.

I sat heavily on the edge of the bed. My shoulders sank.

The man returned to his habit of pacing the room. Despair seemed to envelop us both, accompanying us in the room worse than the smell.

He saw my packet of cigarettes on the desk and asked, with a lift of his chin, 'Can I have one?'

I was surprised at the request. *He* was the one with the gun – we were living by his rules. His strange politeness was disarming.

Slowly, as if my voice might calm an agitated child, I said, 'Sure.'

He took a cigarette and turned to offer me one from the outstretched packet.

'Thanks.'

And there we were. Two people sharing a cigarette. The brand was Camel; the cigarettes were lined up, heads showing, in their distinctive yellow packet with a smiling camel shown in profile, set against pyramids in the background. The packet was soft. He had to tip it forwards into his fingers for the cigarette to come out. He walked to the desk and lit his with the matches placed in the ashtray compliments of the hotel. He passed them to me. I held the cigarette and lit my own, trying not to crush its softness in my fingers.

It was simply the lighting of a cigarette with a gently moving flame. It was an action I had made so many times. In the office in Hong Kong we would stand on the grubby internal office stairs, chatting and smoking, taking a break from being grown-ups. Then it had been to relax and break up the long working day. Now all I felt was my arm as it moved, carrying the cigarette up to my lips and back down again on autopilot.

Ahh.

The familiar taste was there. I knew I was breathing, feeling the smoke passing over my lips. I felt slightly heady. He smoked differently, more like a builder in England, cupping the cigarette in his palm as if he was protecting it from a strong wind.

We became a pair of smokers sharing time. In different circumstances I might have started up a conversation, asked a question, got to know him. This did not happen here. In fact, nothing happened. In the silence, he stood and I sat.

He finished his cigarette first and stubbed it out in the ashtray. I did the same a moment later, standing and then carefully moving past him to the ashtray on the desk. I could see my reflection, like a white ghost, moving towards the window now that it was dark outside. I pressed down on the end of the cigarette, crushing it into the glass tray. Its brown end folded in two by a crease pressed into its middle. The stuffing pushed out of its wrapper.

Then we both heard a noise outside in the corridor.

I said nothing. He said nothing.

I wanted him to forget about me and to think only about himself; maybe then he would trip up, forget to guard me with the gun. Maybe there would be a chance.

We waited. No knock came.

Still nothing happened.

I felt old and homesick. I felt like throwing all of it up.

Then he spoke. He had a plan.

'You will open the door,' he explained, gesturing as if I did not know *exactly* where the door was. 'If anyone ask, we are going to the swimming pool. We are together. We walk to the lift and leave. We go together.'

Actually, his English was OK – better than his plan.

Of course I, handily, still had my swimming costume on under the hotel gown, but even so we would look like the craziest of couples. There would be him in a suit, me in a towelling robe, sandwiched together and mincing towards the gold, reflective lifts.

But I didn't care. His plan meant we would need to open the door.

'Yes, yes, OK,' I said eagerly. The thought of being on the other side of that door was almost too much to hope for.

Heart thumping I stood up and, once again, he placed his body at an angle to my back. I clutched the white towelling material around my tummy. I looked at the door, knowing we were going to open it and try to leave.

I drew down on the shiny handle and the white door began to open. I could feel his body, his breath and the gun as if they were part of me. His smell hung, stagnant, as the door began to open. I was aware of the long corridor to the right. Without turning my head, I was able to see that down it, lining the wall, were a lot of men in khaki clothes. They had guns. They were standing-crouching with their guns all facing the same way – towards the door. Towards us. There were so many of them, like repeating, crouching sprinters waiting for the starter's gun.

I could see them but I knew he couldn't. Not yet.

It was now. It *had* to be now. Sweat and electricity coursed through me.

I reached for my childhood: *come here, wrap around me*. The quietness of my home, the place I had come from. The smell of the sea, with the huge sky above, and Dad and me like tiny dots floating free. Dad, swimming in his big red trunks, and me, my body curling and uncurling as the saltwater passed over my limbs.

I could see Mum with Lucy, Toby and our Labrador, Sam. They were still walking on the beach, crunching over the pebbles, straggled out along the shabby outline of Whitstable beach.

It was all there, *still*, and, then, I let it all go.

CHAPTER 2

THE RUN

Everything went down and into my feet. My legs took over. I gulped at air. *Run, just run. JUST RUN…*

Every muscle clutched to my bones, waiting for the sound of the gun. I knew the bullet would pass right through me, leaving behind a round hole of nothingness. I was ready for it. The centre of my back, just a little lower than between my shoulder blades, was expecting it. A perfect hole you would see right through.

I began to move into the channel of the corridor. I had a chance to live. I had to take it. My body knew it before my mind could explain it.

I ran down the corridor to the left. I was like a scream let loose and bouncing off the walls. Hands were grabbing out to hold me, to stop me, but I could not stop running. Waiting for the shot.

Everyone has a gun. Guns can shoot you. Anyone holding a gun can shoot you.

Behind me, heavy feet shook the corridor as they piled into the room. I heard shots, so many shots, again and again. My body twitched at each sound echoing in the corridor and bouncing around my head. *How can anyone be safe in the midst of all this?*

A small woman in dark blue caught me and tried to steer me into a room on the left. She was strong. I flapped at her like a giant mosquito.

She was there in front of me, talking. I was shaking and jumpy. I was gasping for air as if I'd been held underwater for far too long. She wanted to hold me, to calm me, but I didn't want to be held by anyone. I didn't want to be told what to do. I wanted to be able to move. I wanted to see something I knew, something I could trust.

'Who are you?' I asked her, but I didn't take in her reply.

I had grazes and cuts on my face, arms and back that I couldn't remember getting.

I was half aware that it was all so odd.

After a while, I realised I was sitting on the end of a bed in a room in Jakarta, Indonesia, with someone who was presumably a policewoman. As she spoke, I wondered if her face might be a little like a blowfish.

I felt so stupidly English with goosepimples pricking up on my pale thighs. My swimming costume felt ridiculous. I was aware of my breathing moving my chest up and down, unlike the people surrounding me who were standing solid. I made sure to cover myself up.

I both knew what was happening and was strangely detached from it. It was like having my mind split in two. I was Emma on a business trip, wearing a nice suit, getting ready to meet up with Greg and chat about funding requirements. *So who is this person sitting there looking cold and tired and so confused?* I could see her for a moment, from high above; she was talking words from a mouth, making sounds I did not recognise as my own. I suppose it was the shock.

Later, I sat with two police/army men in a different room in the same hotel, with a theatrical vase of huge flowers. They both had moustaches which moved as they spoke, like a ventriloquist's twitch. They still wore their guns. They had told my work partners on the 'sell side' what had happened and that I would not be meeting them for dinner.

The policemen interviewed me. They wanted to know who I was and why I was there.

I explained, still in my swimming costume and robe. 'My name is Emma Slade. I work in Hong Kong, in finance. I analyse South East Asian companies. We invest in them,' I said to their moustaches. They nodded. 'I am here on a trip arranged by our brokers to meet the companies we invest in.'

I ran out of words. This important job I could no longer understand.

'I had meetings this afternoon. Do you think this might have been connected to them – to my work here in Jakarta?' I too wanted to understand what had happened, to get an explanation.

They noted it all down and then offered what they knew. Firstly they showed me a square, white-edged Polaroid photo. In it the man was slumped against a wall, wearing grubby Y-fronts. Where had his clothes gone – his belt and jacket? Why wasn't he wearing his shoes any more? It was tough to look at. It reminded me of a man I had heard of long ago, left without his clothes, a hostile crowd around him and dark red blood falling down his body. It was a picture of suffering.

The policemen were understandably eager to show me the photo, impressing on me the good job they had done and seeking to reassure me that I was safe now. They talked on.

They said he was a gambler looking for money and that he had some link to Mainland China. Apparently he hadn't known who I was, so we concluded the incident wasn't personal or related to my earlier business meetings. However, they said he had probably been watching me in the hotel before I entered my room. That was a weird thought. To think what else might have been happening, unseen, as I walked up those stairs. *Click clack, click clack.*

They brought out four identical, serrated knives he had been carrying, tucked down into the top of his trousers. They had cream, plastic handles like you might see in a picnic set. They laid them out in a neat line on the glass-topped coffee table. It was the first time I had seen them.

I sat there, quite still, behind the table, looking at the photo I was holding. It was a little bigger than my palm. All it had in it was one man. His head slumped, hanging from his punched-out body, held there in the crease between the wall and the floor. I couldn't stop staring at the photo at the end of my arm. If he wasn't dead, he was in prison. I did not understand how our lives had come to this – how had our paths brought us together to end in this way? The sorrow I felt was overwhelming.

He has to be OK, I thought.

My eyes were still with his body in the photo, but inside I was pleading for reassurance that this broken man was going to recover, that his suffering would only be temporary. I was no longer hearing what the policemen were saying.

But why? Why did I care so much for a man who had held my life at the end of his gun and about whom I knew nothing? I didn't understand so I remained silent. I could not speak this strange wish out loud surrounded, as I was, by my rescuers.

After giving my statement of events to the police, they took me back to my room on the fourth floor. I later found out that this is not recommended in such situations, but it was all a daze to me and I just did what they told me. So I saw how the room was different. I saw the blood on the cream, wallpapered walls, densest on the wall near the door, so incongruous in a hotel room. It streaked downwards, dark red. How could there be so much of it?

I had to collect my things and say if anything was missing. My watch had been returned.

The hotel manager was keen to sort things out. In the room with the flowers, he offered me an air ticket to see my family back in England. I guess I wasn't thinking about the small print at that point. I signed a piece of paper to say I would take no further action on the matter.

The manager arranged for me to move into the hotel's best suite for the night, on the top floor. It was very late at night and there were lots of windows. I am sure the city views would have been stunning on a different occasion.

With crisp pillows propped up behind me, I called Mum back in England from a white-and-gold phone. The time difference was in my favour and I didn't wake her up.

'Mum?' I said. 'Mum, no need to worry. I'm in Jakarta on a business trip. There *was* a man with a gun in my hotel room. I'm OK, but it was very... well, very frightening.' Ever the analyst, considering the right turn of phrase, I wanted my mum to know but not worry too much. Not an easy balancing act to pull off under the circumstances.

I could imagine Mum back in our family home but I didn't dwell on that. I became articulate and business-like in the face of my mother's concern. It's strange when I think back on it. I still cannot believe how sentences-in-the-right-order, breathing-as-normal I was that night. I suppose I had learnt to become quite skilled at shifting my attention to the outside, to the job in hand.

The next morning, I could have gone straight back to Hong Kong or to England, but I wanted to complete the business trip. Perhaps I was in shock but I didn't see any need to leave.

Even so, it was suggested that I move to another hotel. Although there did not appear to be any connection between what had happened and my probing company meetings, no one wanted to take the risk. I moved to a less standout hotel with a small outdoor pool and very few guests.

For the remainder of the trip I was given a bodyguard, an enormous man who had kept many top Indonesian politicians safe. Having his bulk a few feet away, with his short sleeves straining over his muscly upper arms, was reassuring. I am sorry to say I cannot remember his name, just the scale of his shadow. He waited outside as I did two more meetings. The details are a blur to me now but I knew it was always best to get back in the saddle after a fall.

On the next night, the last of the trip, as the sun set behind the cityscape, I sat at the side of the hotel pool. Leisurely I moved my bare toes through the water, feeling the liquid passing over my skin and mixing it with the light. This trip had helped me to envisage the future I was mapping out. I could see it clearly, like being able to look right down to the bottom of the pool beneath my feet.

The racks of suits, the business trips and the thick napkins were lining up ahead of me ready to be put on, walked into it and unfolded with a flourish. I had looked for a moment into the heart of my life and found it shallow, which was rather confusing because this *was* what I had wanted. It was what I had worked so hard to achieve after Dad died. I had turned away from uncertainty and sought career comfort. But now... now what to think?

Still, these were just vague musings and I did not dwell on them. I left them – an emptied cocktail glass sitting by the water with just a little stubborn, fruity scum sticking to the inner edge. I turned my attention to organising my luggage and setting an alarm to make sure I got to the early flight on time.

At the airport the next morning, I thanked the bodyguard and boarded the aircraft back to Hong Kong, my home for the past two years. The journey was as exciting as ever, ending in a blow-the-washing-on-the-line, side-angle descent as the plane banked before landing on the seemingly too-small runway. You really felt you had arrived somewhere. It must be worth it – you'd risked your life to get there! And it was. Hong Kong was on fire.

CHAPTER 3

THE ARRIVAL

I first arrived in Hong Kong in late 1995 for the third of three global placements on the graduate programme of a global bank. HK operated at a speed and level of mental focus I had not experienced before. Money was *the* talking point. Everyone was interested in property prices and the daily movements of the financial markets. The tax rates were low and the jewellery of choice was yellow diamonds. New York, where I had been seconded before Hong Kong, was hurrying along, past windows and no-parking signs, but it did have diversity; museums, art shows, Central Park. Here fast-money-fast was the only sandwich in town.

I expected to hate it but I didn't. I loved its pace and the work focus. It was incessant, passionate, never off your mind; it was either New York with OCD or how I imagined true love to be.

Fast was easy because Hong Kong is a small place so you can fulfil your goals very efficiently. I could see my office from my flat. Underneath my office were a swimming pool to keep fit in and a cafe to eat in. It meant you could achieve a great deal in one day without wasting time on the metro or walking to restaurants. There was just no need to pause.

I did once walk past some older residents gracefully and slowly performing t'ai chi. They were in a small park by a grey office block, close to a busy road. Their knees stayed gently bent as they turned from side to side, their arms slowly moving through the air like sculptors shaping clay. There was no visible conductor but they moved together like a flock of birds making perfect shapes in the sky.

In my down time in Central Hong Kong I went shopping. There was an enormous, gleaming mall called Pacific Place just beside our office. It offered increasingly expensive layers of shopping opportunities. Food was on the ground floor; Versace designer suits were up on the top floor. It was like being slowly seduced: let's get you well fed and then work on your clothes. Let's see how good making money can feel. Let us help you…

I liked being seduced. We all did.

There was another expat from London in the office, Mary-Ann. She was younger than me and beautiful, with natural white-blonde hair and the palest skin. She always looked perfectly air-conditioned. We lived in the same block of flats and Mary-Ann would bring down bottles of vodka to share with my tins of Roses chocolates when we got homesick. Every day we would walk together to work, swim together and have lunch together. It was nice to have her beside me for company. She and Karen, another fund management graduate, were my main friends in the office.

Beyond this friendship group there was a noisy, ready-to-burst energy about being an expat in Hong Kong. It hit you when you went out in the evening. The serious work mood was replaced by loud talk about weekend plans and scuba diving locations; passing over drinks and business cards in quick succession. If possible, I liked to find a quiet seat and relax into it, feeling the sounds banking up like clouds behind a mountain. I might then turn to a Camel on a tough day. Smoking gave me a feeling of confidence, with an air of the unreachable which was helpful in unfamiliar-people situations.

There were a lot of bars of different types to frequent after work if you were in the mood. Some were in the Wan Chai area, where old vegetables were left outside rotting. Some were in the upmarket hotels of Central, where beautifully crafted snacks with glossy outsides came automatically, without being ordered. Being of the rather tame persuasion, Mary-Ann and I tended to be at the latter more than the former.

On a Friday after work, I might meet up with Bruce, a friend in commercial banking, or perhaps my cousin Edward, in a bar in Central. Edward was in corporate finance, where people seemed bred to compete and were very clear about their life goals.

These times and settings caught my attention for a while but occasionally I found myself drifting off, recalling the wiggly path I had taken to be standing in a bar in Hong Kong surrounded by lots of loud people as a transparent bead of sweat slowly traced a path down my cleavage.

Despite my childhood garden musings with Dad as things developed I had put the idea of a career in finance firmly to the back of my mind. Until Dad's illness I had increasingly imagined I would be an artist or a curator; nothing so conventional and dull as banking! But, with his death, I could not continue with that plan. I needed to stand up. I needed to make sure I could make a living and not lean on Mum. I needed to not waste my life but make a definite success of it. Most of all, I wanted to hear again 'We're so proud of you, Em' – and I wanted the hug that went with it.

I genuinely thought that everything would be OK after Jakarta; that I would be able to put it all quietly behind me. At most I thought I might suffer some temporary volatility and then revert to the mean. It honestly did not occur to me that what happened in that hotel room would turn out to be so hard to recover from.

I had been through Dad's death, various strains at university and exam pressures in the job. I thought that I'd had an unusual experience which would naturally lead to fear and some concerns, but that these feelings would fade away over time. Compared to Dad's death, which was devastating and from which I truly didn't think I'd recover, this event was shocking but over. Or so I thought.

But maybe things had piled up already. Perhaps Jakarta was just the little star that gets carefully placed on the top of a delicate sculpture of sugar and air. It's often the last thing that causes a beautiful artifice to collapse. Poetic, yes – and if only it had been that simple.

Although no one had diagnosed it yet, I was developing post-traumatic stress disorder (PTSD) and *disorder* is definitely what it felt like.

I began to suffer flashbacks, as I now know to call them. In the bright daylight of a Hong Kong park full of flowers and wedding couples being photographed by lily pads in ponds, I was filled with fear. I was running down corridors, feeling gun metal in my skin, carpet strands stuck to my face.

Men reaching into their jacket pockets for wallets would cause me to cower. People moving fast towards me would cause me to shout out or strangle a sound in my throat.

Everything became increasingly disordered, particularly in the dimension of time. The word 'flashback' is not embodied enough to convey the experience I was going through. Indeed, in other instances, the word 'flashback' might refer to a previous time in quite a mundane, even positive way. In the case of PTSD, the flashback is an overwhelming thing that occurs in the present and never stops, so you are in a past-present moment *all* the time. It's always running in the background, like the 'musak' my mum hates playing in the background in shops. Sometimes you notice it a lot; sometimes it's just there droning on.

Sitting at my desk in Hong Kong, there were the usual telephones, screens and broker reports in front of me, but there was something weaving itself into the office landscape, leaving an only-just-visible trail of slime across the surfaces.

What's that?

A door shutting, outside in the corridor.

I can smell him. My heart is beating fast. I can feel it, so loud.

But of course it's nothing.

'Emma, have you got Amanda's research for the next Global Investment meeting?'

I need to bend down and hide. Quick, Emma, quick. Hide.

'Yes, Michael, I have it here,' I heard a part of myself saying, picking up a document as I felt cold sweat on my neck and my shoulders stiffening. 'The main thing is the property situation in Japan. She thinks things might be improving.'

The rancid smell and creak of shoes…

'Load of crap,' came Michael's quick response as he pressed…

… closer…

buttons on his Bloomberg screen showing a bright yellow graph heading south.

… and closer.

'Back in a mo,' I said, determined to sound casual.

I went to the bathroom just to be alone and wipe my hands, face and armpits like a modern-day Lady Macbeth, repeating actions, hoping to scrub away any remaining trace.

It's OK, it's OK. It's going to be… it will be OK.

The bathroom was the easiest place to escape to at work. Gripping the sides of the sink, I would look straight at my eyes in the mirror as if it would help me to outstare my insides.

If it sounds bonkers – well, I did tell you it was a disordering, and it was heading straight at me, between the eyeballs, like a torpedo locked on its prey, all while I would be answering Michael's queries on fund management.

Again and again, my muscles tensed going through their paces. I had to brace, be on my guard. Prepare. Prepare to run. Find the exit, see the exit, go. I was an animal, hunted by my own mind. I was both the baddie and the victim, both the hostage and the hostage taker. It was a boxing match which lasted all day long, without a referee.

OK, I was in the office sitting at a desk, and of course other people were there, but what I felt was alone. What I felt was trapped and my body was in terror.

At night I would wake. The sweat of my hands would leave prints on the wall by the bed. I was terrified by the movement of light across the horizontal blinds. When you're scared of the dark *and* of daylight, things get rather tricky.

As I was later told, these extended periods of stress responses at such a raised level take a toll on the chemical body which is hard to fully recover from. I did not know it then but finite chemicals such as serotonin were being quickly depleted; a permanent change in my composition. A drastic reduction in serotonin or an impaired ability to produce further serotonin through experiences of trauma is thought to link to depression. So science says that high stress levels are linked to depression, the boom and bust of the mind world.

The most notable long-term, permanent effect of the PTSD for me has been the negative impact it has had on my memory and ability to remember facts, something which I had previously been so capable of. Even now I clutch out in vain as a name falls, invisible, around me; another silent feather. I am reminded of those left frail in an old people's home or of the graceful t'ai chi dancers on Hong Kong lawns, all silently shaping air with their hands.

It happened slowly at first, but eventually I stopped being able to recognise the person I was. It became increasingly hard to live in my own skin. I tried. I really tried. Like a little girl screwing up her eyes and clenching her fists. I still thought I could make it all OK. You see, I am definitely a determined person and I had channelled my determination into being a success. When I was offered the place on the graduate programme, I was focused. I wanted to understand the numbers and the economics and the way it all worked. Apart from Love, it seemed that Money was the most important thing in the grown-up world. I was certain that if I applied myself I *would* be able to understand it all.

After successful placements in the London and New York offices, I had joined the emerging market debt team in Hong Kong. This area of investment was quickly developing in South East Asia so I was joining an exciting, cutting-edge area of investment. There was always a buzz about this desk in comparison to the quieter equity desk. I became a South East Asian emerging debt analyst and all I had to do was complete the final set of the Chartered Financial Analyst exams I had been swotting away for alongside work and I would be *that plus* a CFA.

In Hong Kong at this point, investments came from a wide range of countries but Indonesia and Thailand were key, and sectors included anything from petroleum to concrete manufacturing to telephone development. The South East Asian markets in the 1990s seemed to offer the Holy Grail of investment possibility. Small, developing companies in Asia were at the take-off point of the business cycle – all they needed was capital to back them, and in we came. We were The Investors, with swagger and big-shouldered suits. In the end, the newness of these markets and the lack of in-depth research on them were like small pieces of ice gradually settling under the surface, building up, as we carried on above, playing in sunlight so bright it blinded our vision.

Our emerging market debt team was headed up by Michael, a friendly, enthusiastic American fund manager. I liked that he was always getting up and down from his seat, turning to a screen, picking up a phone, walking to the trading desk, smiling. He said, 'OK, OK' and 'yeah, yeah' a lot, mostly when he was in the midst of listening to you and doing something else at the same time. He breathed out multitasking, distracted happiness in a market which was going his way.

Michael would twirl on his seat, showing me the spreadsheet listing our investments. 'Hey, Emma, d'ya see that? Double digit returns; now tell me where else you can find that?' He was lightheaded with the joy of such juicy investments looking back at him from the screen. If he had moved any more, it would have made me dizzy.

I so enjoyed being part of this upswing, led by my boss. Michael and I got on well. We were both inquisitive, competitive in nature and were the two expats on the team. He was American of Irish descent; I was British from the Home Counties. He wore open shirts and slip-on shoes; I wore subtle pinstripes and understated jewellery. Generally I was less bold, certainly on the social front, but I had my moments and I felt we understood each other most of the time.

In July 1996, I had my birthday in a restaurant called Don Juan in Lan Kwai Fong, but my memory of the full details is a little fuzzy. I know it was a noisy, crowded affair, gatecrashed by various expat friends of expats. I was feeling good in my black Max Mara trousers with tasteful but cheeky zips for pockets. At some point there was a wobbly conga round the tables, a loud group rendition of 'All Along the Watchtower' and I was pronounced to be officially thirty. Somehow I wandered back to my flat in the early hours. I was skew-whiff, carrying my high, strappy sandals with a carefree swing. Anyone could see: I had finally made my life a real success.

CHAPTER 4

THE ICEBERG

Which is how I ended up going to meetings in Jakarta in September 1997. Before that trip though a few things were to change in the landscape of South East Asian markets.

As was clear from my thirtieth birthday party, towards the end of a good do, the dancers begin to trip over each other's feet and stumble as the intoxication takes hold. The lights seem so, so bright when they suddenly come on and you begin to hear the long, sharp hiss of deflating balloons as they whirr crazily round the room before shrivelling to a sudden death on the floor. Eventually, someone sweeps them up and puts them in the bin.

And, in the early hours, we all remember that unavoidable truth: the bigger the party the greater the hangover. This is how it was when, in July 1997, the Asian Financial Crisis emerged from behind the shadows and we all started to reach for the aspirin.

Financial markets are often quiet and illiquid during the summer months as people take their holiday and July 1997 was no exception to this norm. In addition, HK was being handed over to China, to create the Hong Kong Special Administrative Region. The 1st and 2nd of July were made public holidays to celebrate this event, adding to the sleepiness of the financial markets.

On the morning of the 2nd, I walked down to see the Chinese soldiers now stationed near the waterfront in Hong Kong. Their faces looked set and they wore bright white gloves as they made their formal movements back and forth. I stared for a while and then went back to normality at the office. I had nothing particular to do so I was happy to loll about the office looking at Reuters and Bloomberg news feeds before deciding how to spend the rest of my day off. Because I was single and Hong Kong was such a work-orientated culture, days off and weekends could get a bit dull. Bruce and I might go walking in north Kowloon but that weekend he was busy with visitors from England, there to see the handover.

Sitting in the office that day, the news came through that Thailand had devalued its currency, breaking its reassuring peg to the US dollar. The newsfeeds became rapid and red in colour. The impact was immediate, with the Thai baht devaluing by 20 per cent and the government requesting help from the International Monetary Fund (IMF). Imagine getting in a lift and it hurtling straight down – *thud* – to the basement. That was the Thai baht. If you looked down the lift shaft you could see it there – a currency in distress.

Over the next few weeks, all the Asian currencies began devaluing and asset values declined dramatically, particularly assets that had been valued in the country's domestic currency – as our investments had been. By mid-August, the pressure on the Indonesian rupiah became too great and the currency was allowed to float freely, no longer propped up by Central Bank interventions, and it plunged in value. Around 30 per cent of our portfolios were invested in Indonesian rupiah assets.

'Oh shit,' as Michael said – a lot.

Soon we were to discover a truth not often stressed in financial analysis textbooks: 'value' only exists when someone is prepared to buy your investment. Our screens showed 'values' which halved overnight yet remained pure theory because no one wanted to buy them at any price in reality. You often read that markets are driven by fear and greed. We had been in headlong greed mode and then we had experienced the emergency stop when everything came to a halt, incapacitated by fear.

When people are scared they freeze. Then they panic and want to do something to make it better. They want to run. It's understandable – it's called your sympathetic nervous system response and it's hardwired into human beings. Soon investors wanted out. This was painful given the tough market conditions and appalling prices. Michael dealt with it. He had bouts of frenzied activity and swearing at the currency policy decisions of various countries.

As the surface values of the investments dissolved, more of the iceberg that had lingered quietly under the surface became visible. With hindsight and rigorous, retrospective accounting rules, it was easy to see why things had panned out in this way.

The speed at which supposedly successful businesses fell apart was astounding. In a click, paper accounts turned to fiction, telephone numbers to dead sounds. If these young markets had been well researched and highly diversified maybe it would have been different. They had been dubbed 'the Tigers' but perhaps we were arrogant to imagine ourselves as masters of the circus.

Michael and I flew to Tokyo at short notice. We needed to speak to our investors face-to-face. It was crucial to keep them in the loop and do some hand-holding. It was my first trip to Japan. From what I glimpsed between meetings, it is a stunning country of incredible detail and precise manners. But then again my main contact was with the hotel reception.

The main meeting of the trip was unusual in that everyone smoked throughout and everyone in the room, besides me, was a man. We all sat round a horseshoe-shaped table; Michael and I side by side in the middle. We did well, explaining our investments and the macroeconomic situation as best we could given it was all a moving target. It was, however, hard to know who in the room to concentrate on, who the main decision makers were. There was a rumour the company rotated staff through jobs on a three-yearly cycle and that the man currently making the key decisions was about to leave. We weren't even sure if his replacement was one of the attendees. It wasn't just the smoke that created an air of fogginess.

That evening Michael and I unwound together in a bar, high up in the hotel, relieved we had managed to stall any further action from the Japanese investors. The bar had a long glass window looking out over the city, ready to be used in a Hollywood movie. We sat and chatted, drinking transparent sake from thin ceramic containers. We ate beautifully constructed snacks, their elements brought together to look like flowers settled on a plate of leaves. As we relaxed we allowed ourselves to feel a sense of 'us against the world', battling the evil forces of the markets and doing our best for our investors and the fund. It was good to rekindle the old feeling of comradeship and pleasant to forget the strains of the office and feel a moment of shared success; a bit like the old days.

I would have preferred to return from Japan to better news, to something going our way, but that just was not happening. I went to see Watachak Publishing in Bangkok (Michael loved the name and had a habit of repeating it as if it was a type of fried chicken: 'Watachak, Watachak. Hey, Emma, how 'bout that Watachak?!') as I was concerned about their financial health.

The company's balance sheet had not been in a strong position – even before the currency crisis – so I went to Bangkok to see for myself. I arrived at their office as desks and chairs were being taken out through the front door. Inside, young Thai office staff were swinging their slim legs off the remaining tables. No one seemed to be in charge or know exactly where the furniture was going. That was our money being walked out of the door to an unknown destination.

Watachak was written off.

Back in the office in Hong Kong, I watched as screens of red numbers and blank spaces multiplied.

At one point the phone rang and it was an Indonesian businessman. 'Money, we need money. Please help us,' he said. I suspected the caller ran a government-backed building business. I thought he might be crying, or drunk. Stunned, I paused to digest and, in that time, he hung up.

It was at this point that I decided to go to Jakarta to see what was happening to our Indonesian investments. Michael felt that if the companies had government backing, which they often did, they must be OK. I was more sceptical. No one knew. South East Asia had not been in this position before.

I would go on my own, but there would be two sell-side brokers from other companies who would set up the meetings and accompany me to them. In more normal circumstances sell-side brokers would be hoping to gain new business from such investor trips but at this point it was more about soothing waters and hand-holding. One of these brokers was a tall dark American called Greg who worked for Bear Sterns, the bank which collapsed on the back of the US subprime mortgage crisis in 2008. I had been out for a couple of dinners with him a couple of times and had wondered, in the back of a shared cab, if he actually wanted to ask me out. Sell-side-buy-side links could be complex though. He never asked and I never let my head rest on his shoulder late at night.

I took an early flight to Jakarta on 3 September. Jakarta is an hour behind Hong Kong so Greg organised for my minimal luggage to be dropped off at the hotel and we went straight off to a full schedule of company meetings. I had ratios and numbers right on my tongue. I was ready to ask some serious questions. I wanted evidence of assets written on the company balance sheets. I wanted to know less about the future and more about the Right Here, Right Now. What I wanted was to be shown The Truth.

The meetings were not reassuring but I felt I had done well at clearing some wool from our eyes. There was a little good, some bad and there was definitely going to be a lot of ugly. Despite this, performing well as an analyst was a good feeling; it was my job.

I checked in at the large reception desk of the Grand Hyatt Hotel, Jakarta, and went to sit in the mezzanine lounge area, looking down on the reception below as people went back and forth. Savouring a cappuccino and a dry Italian biscuit, with my laptop beside me, I enjoyed watching other people doing stuff and ticking things off their own 'urgent' lists.

From there I finished the coffee, picked up my computer and felt my hips move and heels click as I began my walk towards my hotel room; a luxurious end to a big day in Asia.

PLANTING THE SEED

The most powerful part of Jakarta was not the fear or the hurt – although there was much of that. It was the deep feeling of compassion and care I felt at seeing the photo of the man. This feeling, coming out of a sewer of an experience, planted a seed in the mud which was to become the most powerful and helpful part of the whole thing. My capacity to care for that other human being, even while he had caused me pain and fear, was a huge surprise to me.

o

CHAPTER 5

THE CRACK

After Jakarta, the market dominos continued to tip forwards, the momentum now unstoppable. Despite the IMF packages, the Asian economies continued to worsen, particularly in Indonesia.

I had gone on to a local work contract in Hong Kong which meant my original mini-flat with wall-to-wall mirrors in Lan Kwai Fong had become too pricey so I needed to find another place within walking distance of work. Given the all-consuming nature of work, I didn't have a lot of time to weigh up the options and quickly plumbed for a flat-share with a Texan named Wes Wesley who had advertised for a flatmate. His flat was on the edge of Lan Kwai Fong, on the first floor of a building, its front windows closed to the efforts of the dry cleaners below.

I guess I hadn't paid enough attention when I first looked round. I should have taken note of all the steam coming up from the dry cleaners below, making the flat appear in patches of cloudy smoke like a baddie walking on stage in a pantomime.

Wes had a large selection of different-coloured cowboy boots neatly lined up on the inside of the front door. He ate a lot of chicken legs and digestive biscuits and had a big exercise structure in the middle of the flat with pulleys and levers.

Wes, I discovered, wanted a girlfriend and had been looking at magazines which offered to pair people up with people in other countries. After four weeks in the flat, Wes invited a woman from Ukraine over and decided he therefore no longer wanted a flatmate. One night Wes took my laptop while I slept in my room and threatened not to give it back if I did not leave. Such is the power of passion.

I called Bruce and he helped me move out at top speed. Luckily Karen and Russell had a large flat on Kennedy Road and, while I regrouped, I stayed there with them.

Karen was a lovely person; kind and softly spoken. She came from outside Edinburgh and now was working hard as an equity analyst at a desk further down from mine. She lived with Russell, who was from Northern Ireland; a clever strategist working for Credit Lyonnais and happy to admit his fondness for pork pies. Karen and I had initially met on a graduate training week back in England and struck up an easy friendship. Now, in Hong Kong, and officially engaged to Russell, she would often relax with me and a Baileys and ice, leaving the doors to their balcony open on the more humid nights. It was some sanctuary from my own head as well as a safe place to stay post-Wes Wesley.

The question of whether to remain in Hong Kong was lurking in my mind but I still *liked* my job and wanted to do it well. The vision of an endless conveyor belt of suits I had glimpsed sitting by the pool in Jakarta had been overtaken by the day-to-day challenge of working in the midst of PTSD. It was easier not to think about me and try to focus on the currencies, portfolios and investors. They were definitely a serious distraction.

I wasn't the only one wondering about my place in Hong Kong. Our office was witnessing a dwindling number of expats. Since the tanks had come over the border to mark the handover of Hong Kong to China, many were rethinking their career plans.

After a particularly tiring week in late December, I went on a trip to Lantau Island, which is a well-known visitor attraction. I went with one of the other new graduates, a smart American woman with long, red curly hair; she stood out beautifully in the Hong Kong scenery. She walked like a Pre-Raphaelite.

Lantau Island is home to an enormous (34 m high) seated Buddha, reached by walking up 268 steps. On that day it was warm and crowded. At the base of these steps people milled around near the large pots of incense which came to waist height on me, their curved metal legs supporting wide bowls of sand into which tall incense sticks had been stuck and lit. These sticks were nearly two feet long, with strong red wooden stems and yellow incense packed around the central support like a yellow bulrush plant. They didn't look all that natural but were effective in creating a powerful scent.

There was much to see below and around this statue after the climb up but we were finding the crowds a bit intense. People were bustling and taking photos and calling out to each other in sounds we could not translate, so all we heard was shouting. It was not quite what we had hoped for.

Away from the statue I wandered off and found a quiet room in a separate building, the polished wooden floor shining with light from a wall of intricately carved windows. There was a small shrine. It took me a few moments to realise there was a man in grey-blue, formal clothes (I supposed they were monastic robes of some type) sitting cross-legged on a simple wooden chair. He was sitting by the wall just to one side of the windows so the light fell to his right and he remained sheltered in a more shadowed space. His head was slightly tilted down and I did not want to stare to see if his eyes were open or closed. He was not asleep; he was doing something in a non-doing type of way. So shiny was the floor, his presence was gently reflected in it.

The sight of him sitting in his quiet stillness was entrancing. In his company I began to feel it was time to go.

Back in the office that week there were frequent calls from our investors. Michael was putting out fires and shouting at screens a fair bit. He was blustering and I had the feeling his marriage was not going so well. I had never met his wife but I knew she existed. I noticed that, at times, he turned his chair away from the desk to take a call. I noticed he would speak quietly – this was very unusual for him – one hand coming up to cup the phone in a way he never did when he was shooting the breeze on calls with brokers. I always gave him a moment or two after these calls before turning to ask him a question or round him up for a meeting.

Michael went on a business trip to explore new opportunities in India. While he was away his boss from the London office, an older man with a traditional over-the-head-combed hairstyle, came to visit and see for himself how things were going. His name was Jim. He was a reasonable man. Jim had worked in the industry for a long time. Later, when I left the bank, he wistfully told me he too would also like to resign but he had maintenance to pay and school fees to think of. He was in for the duration. His coat was tired and in need of a decent clean.

I was evidently working hard on the desk, fielding queries and decisions as portfolio revaluations brought tougher and tougher news. Jim decided we should have a chat. In a quiet room with a glass wall, so you could watch people walking past to the coffee machine, the two of us sat down on the same side of a large, wooden oval table with phones on it and a screen at one end.

'I'm very impressed by what you're doing here, Emma, but you do seem to have a lot of job roles – a lot on your shoulders.'

'Well, it *is* a lot but it's OK.'

'And now Michael's away…' Jim prompted, leaning in.

'Yes, I wish he was here but India is looking really interesting. It's OK, he'll be back soon.'

'And what about the latest on the portfolios? Are clients talking to you directly?'

'Some, but Michael does most of that.'

'Right, I see. Well, good job and good luck with the end-of-year reports. I'll have a chat with Michael at the global meeting.' He seemed to be making a mental note to himself out loud.

'OK, great. Thanks,' I said, thinking it had hardly been a lengthy chat.

Jim returned to London and Michael came back from India all fired up about education systems and cheap labour.

It was approaching the time of the office Christmas party. In the world of finance December is often appraisal time when bonuses are decided, and February/March is when they hit your bank account; our bank followed this model. Performance and pay were absolutely linked and your boss was the key decider of how good a bonus you would get based on your past year's performance. Bonuses can easily become the subject of months of speculation and jostling for position.

Michael had already given me the highest mark possible in a written appraisal sent to HQ before he went to India, before I had met with Jim, so I wasn't thinking a lot about it. Michael told me that before he left and of course I was very pleased. Top marks meant a good bonus. I had passed the last set of CFA exams and, on the back of low income tax rates in Hong Kong, had bought a house in England and was keen to get the mortgage down.

Michael zipped straight off to the Global Investment Forum in London and I didn't see him for a further couple of weeks. By the time Michael returned it was late December and the last afternoon he would be in the office before his return to the US for the Christmas holidays.

Our formal verbal appraisal and bonus chat had been set in the diary for some time, scheduled in advance due to his travel plans. I was feeling rather lousy; an end-of-year head cold adding a red nose above the black suit and slowness to my brain. I hadn't thought much about the meeting, imagining we'd have a jokey chat then I would retire back home to take some paracetamol.

Outwardly still Emma, inside I was my own distressed asset; sleep deprived and haunted by a thin Indonesian ghost, increasingly going rancid in my mind. Coping with that and falling assets in the portfolio was plenty. I had no time or mental energy for reflecting on office complications and form filling.

It was good to have Michael back in the office and know that The Boss was overseeing things. As usual all day he had been rushing in and out, caught up in his own whirlwind. I tied up loose ends on my desk as the office slowly emptied, the staff bored by the depressing financial markets and keen to get some feel-good factor from the Christmas holidays.

Michael finally returned to his desk and said, 'Shall we?'

'Sure,' I said, and grabbed a spiral notepad and pen in case we had to chat through future plans.

I followed him to a small office away from the open-plan one we usually sat in. He seemed a little less chatty than normal but, hey, what did I know – he was a moody guy.

I closed the door after us and sat down opposite him. It was the first time we had really looked each other in the eye for a while. I smiled and got ready for my end-of-year pat on the back.

Face to face and out it came.

'Who are you? What the hell do you think you are doing, stabbing me in the back to Jim?'

'What?' was all I had time to get out.

'You,' he threw back. 'You've put my job on the line in London.' He was red faced right up to the curls on his head. I thought he might froth at the mouth. 'It's *your* fault.'

It was not a physical blow – there was a large desk between us – but it felt like it. I had been holding things together with the smallest pieces of gnarled Blu-Tack, seeking to complete tasks, analyse information and, most importantly, to Please My Boss. This boss: the very one that was shouting at me, furious. *What is he even talking about?*

'But I haven't done anything. Honestly, Michael. I don't understand. What have I done?'

'Don't give me that crap. Just *don't* give me that crap. You know exactly what you've done.' His spit shot across the desk, so large it had bubbles. I did not flinch; it was the least of my worries.

Inside I felt my body freeze in the confusion but my heart was beating so fast. I just had not seen any of this coming. I genuinely did not feel I had done anything wrong. I did not think I had stabbed him in the back. I thought I had been running round working really hard saving his butt from some of the crap decisions he had made and didn't want to deal with. Somehow, between Jim's visit to Hong Kong and Michael's visit to London, two and two must have had a baby and made five.

'Just go,' he screamed at me.

Totally dazed, I did as he said.

That was it: my appraisal – done.

My bonus was already in the system, too late to be pulled back no matter how much he shouted. How could I have got a number one and been in so much trouble? It made no sense. I had been seen as Snow White.

On this dark and drizzly evening I went back to the flat on autopilot.

I sat down heavily on the sofa, confused and trying to think straight with a foggy head. I was sneezing-angry-worried-weary.

No part of the world made any sense to me any more.

Trust, loyalty, faith, belief – all crushed by these events. Was there anything left in Hong Kong worth staying for?

Christmas passed in a blur of a dribbly cold and the hot sweats that went with them. Waking up at the start of 1998 and a return to work, I began my usual morning routine, getting dressed for the office. Feeling the soft silk of my light blue shirt as I put it on, slipping its delicate buttons into their openings. Over that went the reassuring structure of a tailored grey suit with just a slight sheen to it, its weight resting on my shoulders. Standing there, just for a moment, like a whisper, I felt the morning air come through the open windows of the flat and brush my face.

I left the flat and took the usual walk to the office but something had changed. I had to act now.

At my desk I wasted no time. I sent an internal computer message to the CEO, who had an office further down the open-plan room. His name was Bob. I hadn't had much to do with him previously but, with Michael in the US and not communicating with me, I messaged Bob. Still trying to keep the surface calm as evening water waiting for the setting sun, I chose my words carefully.

Bob, I feel I have done well putting the events of Jakarta behind me but I realise now that I do wish to return to my home in the UK as soon as possible.

My head was saying: 'I can't take any more and I need to leave now.'

I thought he would realise I meant urgently, no delay. *Now*, Bob. But he didn't. My message was articulate and apparently well considered, not the ramblings of an ex-hostage who had been trashed by their boss just before Christmas.

Back came the reply: *Really pleased with how you are doing. Let's review later in the spring. Best Bob.*

Best Bob.

Not best, Bob. Not at all, not in the slightest, not by any stretch of the imagination, Bob.

I sat at my desk looking at the message in disbelief. Had he not understood what I had written? I never usually say what I want, but look, Bob, this time I have. Surely you can see I mean now – not later, not spring daffodils, not any time other than *right now*.

As the words sunk in, time slowed. I turned off the computer, got up deliberately, moving through space as if heavy, with boots full of sand. I walked at a precise pace to see Karen. She sat on the oval-shaped Asian equities desk, a few tables down, with her fellow equity specialists. Since it was her flat I had been staying in since Jakarta she knew something of the night sweats and hidden behaviour.

I leaned over her right shoulder. 'I'm leaving right now. I'm going to the lifts,' I whispered the words into her fleshy ear. I was being very careful as I thought my whisper might turn into a scream if I did not use this measured control.

I began to walk away, heading out of the office doors for the shiny golden lifts that were my new gateway to freedom.

Karen ran after me and tried to grab my arm, to hold me back.

But there was no holding me. I pulled away and went quickly out to the lifts. I stared at my warped reflection in the lift doors. They were closed. Sudden desperation overtook me. I pushed my fingers into the slot where they joined and tried to open them with my hands. I pushed at the button too but mostly I tried to manually separate the lift doors. I had to get out; I had to run. The urge to run was too strong.

Karen tried to restrain me, putting her arms around my shoulders.

'Stop it, stop it,' I said to her. 'I'm going to the airport. I have to go. I have to go home now.' A sob was rising up. I could no longer stop it. I could not look at her but I could feel her arms.

'It's OK, Emma. It's OK. Go to the flat. I'll shut down my computer and come right now. Right now. Just wait for me. OK?' Karen said with her soft Edinburgh accent.

I turned round to see the kindness on her face.

Karen – my friend. I trusted her. I knew she cared.

Inside I began to collapse in slow motion, like a building being dynamited from below.

'OK?' she repeated, looking at me.

'Yes, OK,' I said, thankful for her guidance as the ash and debris began to fall and my face turned grey.

The lift came, the doors separated of their own accord and I got in. As the doors were re-closing she waited to smile goodbye.

Thank you, Karen.

I headed back to the flat on Kennedy Road, stutter-running through Hong Kong Park, past the ornamental flowers and the people moving in the other direction. I passed the company's finance officer, who looked rather surprised to see me, his expression of confusion staying with me as –

over tall and out of place – I moved on in a way a suited businesswoman with precisely placed lipstick should not. My inside state was separating from its outside container. Even I could see that now.

At the flat I was just so tired. Any capacity to 'keep it going' had dissipated. I looked around for something to pack. It had to be something that mattered. Most things I cared nothing about and I was happy to leave it all behind.

Except: I picked up my statue of a monk found in a cluttered antiques shop in Hong Kong. He had travelled over from Thailand, his head bowed, his hands resting together in prayer at his heart. As is common in Thailand he is sitting on his heels, not cross-legged as is usual in India and the Himalayas. This monk has his robes carved as part of him, then painted russet red. Little black curls on his head recall the act of the Buddha cutting his hair off, symbolising the severing of his links to the material world and the ego. What was left were small, carved coils like ammonites painted black, showing the shape of his head. The lack of hair made his two ears stand out, giving him the look of someone sitting but listening intently. I had a small, black, Antler hand-luggage bag ideal for short business trips abroad. I wrapped a towel around him. I laid him in there on his back, sitting on his carved lotus-flower base. Zipping it around, I closed the bag shut. I was ready for the airport.

Karen and Russell returned to the flat not long after. I was still breathing fast and heavy as if I had been running a marathon within the tight walls of their flat.

They convinced me to eat some mushroom soup and said I had to speak to someone before going to explain what had happened with Michael, to make it clear why I had to leave now. They knew the bank had paid for me to see a counsellor after Jakarta and said I should ring her. *I* didn't think I needed to explain anything to anyone; not now I had finally said it. *Enough. I have had enough.*

But Karen and Russell called the counsellor and I agreed to go. Sitting in her small office that same day, I recounted the details of the performance review and the message to Bob. I stated my absolute certainty that now I had to go home. The post-Jakarta counselling sessions had involved a fair amount of chatting about markets and Michael as the continued strain of work merged with earlier incidents. She was aware that things had not been easy since Jakarta. The counsellor wrote a fax to the bank setting out the situation. She said this was a good thing to do. She wanted to get the facts of the previous days on paper.

With that done, I returned to the flat, took my bag with my monk and went to the airport. It was wonderful to feel the shakes and bumps of the plane, the pull upwards, and then to know for absolute certain that the plane had left the ground. It was a fact. I was getting away from it all. Everything would be OK now.

Sitting next to me in business class was an older expat lady. She was well tanned and heavily jewelled, with little vertical lines of skin gathering above the buttons of her open shirt. She ordered gin and tonics throughout the flight. I wondered what she did with the rest of her life. With so much stuff on her and care taken over her appearance, why was she drinking so much? I never found out – she was not that chatty despite having such a colourful shirt.

I was to discover later that, while I was in the air en route to London, a great deal of something smelly hit the fan when that fax rolled out from the machine to sit on someone's desk in London. I didn't know and I certainly no longer cared. Looking down, you know the people are still running, still negotiating, getting things from one another, cramming their heads with facts; as you lift further up, all these people and their needs and hopes become dots, like Braille on paper.

I arrived back in England in the freezing cold. It was early January 1998 and I had been away for nearly three years.

CHAPTER 6
THE RETURN

Back in England I moved into my mortgaged house. It was in Faversham, about fifteen minutes' drive from Whitstable, where my mother and brother, Toby, were still living. My sister, Lucy, had moved to the outskirts of Faversham with her husband, Kevin, and they were expecting their first child.

My brown trunk arrived from Hong Kong; Karen and the office must have packed it up and sent it on. I took out books on statistics, silver-framed photos, Aretha Franklin CDs, examining them like a curator handling ancient artefacts. Most precious of all came my second statue. The companion to the meditating monk; a praying nun, her hands in the centre of her chest and her head bowed. Only the different swell of the torso indicating that the statue represents a female practitioner. I got her out and set them side by side again. It was good to see them.

I bought a big ficus plant to share my new home with. These beautiful plants with woven trunks are in the family of the fig species. The sacred fig tree has become known as the Bodhi Tree; the tree under which the man who was to become known as the Buddha gained enlightenment in Bodh Gaya, Northeast India. It is said that, after his Enlightenment, the Buddha spent a whole week in front of the tree, standing with unblinking eyes, gazing at it with gratitude. I knew none of this then; I just knew I wanted *that* tree whose bark looked like it was made from streams of frozen water.

I bought a telescope for the top bedroom in order to look at the moon. I drank a bit. I got confused and thought I had bought a car and found I hadn't. My memory was very strange. The full extent of the disordering was becoming clear. I don't know *why* exactly but now I could not read or write. The black squiggles on the paper gave me intense headaches. My mum had to do it for me, reading out my post to me like bedtime stories.

It was like re-entry from outer space. I looked at my sister. She was so excited, her small frame beamed as she displayed her first pregnancy; this would be Mum's first grandchild. Of course life had carried on for her and for the others. Lucy had got married while I was in Hong Kong and was developing the family life she had always wanted.

It was so hard to relax and join in. The constant state of fear was always running through me. My empathy skills were at an all-time low – how can you put yourself in the place of another when you are so lost yourself? I must have seemed selfish and disinterested.

I was furious if anyone was late, if they looked like they might not turn up or let me down. It became very, very hard to distinguish what was a threat and what was not. This was the anger, and after the anger settled down what it left behind was a disconnected sense of loss like a floating despair.

Physically I was pale and thin. The beautiful turquoise of my swimming costume and the confidence to demand more towels seemed a long way back. I was shrunken, like one of those peat-bog bodies. In the cold of England I took to wearing three layers to keep warm.

It must have been worrying for Mum to see me in this way. At the time it was so hard to talk though, for both of us; neither of us wanting to make too much of it.

We would meet for walks in the nearby woods, Mum with carrier bags tucked into her bumbag, ready to be pulled out after the dog did his business, and a whistle around her neck. She had a waterproof jacket, boots and a keen eye for puddles of disgusting water the dog was bound to want to roll in. Satchmo was a huge Newfoundland dog named after Louis Armstrong, a jazz musician Mum and Dad both loved. He happily sprayed the world around him with slobber. *He* was the one who needed the treats and the endless supply of towels.

Mum loves animals; she says they are easier than people – which I can see. She grew up in Hampshire with horses and two chow chows. She had gone to a kind of finishing school and learnt deportment. It was funny to see her now, with her whistle and carrier bags, fending off drool. She had already moved far away from her roots of pearl necklaces and correct pronunciation.

We all let go of things. We have to. Like snakes, if we don't shed skins as we grow, we risk suffocating within ever-tighter casing, strangling our own throats, repeating the same sentences over and over again.

My life up to that point seemed to have involved a lot of skin-shedding, or 'change', as Mum would say in a mildly despairing tone as if it was a particularly dangerous verb. She may have had to do some of it in her transition from

Hampshire to Kent but I seemed to 'positively invite' it in. And that did not seem to be A Good Thing as, at that stage, it was hard to see how change was anything other than a way of definitely screwing things up. Jakarta fitted the pattern of me giving it my best shot but not seeing it through. Blast.

Trying to work out how to fit into things or make them fit to me, or something like that, had not proved super easy so far, even before Jakarta.

I was the eldest of three and, therefore, the first to forge the path. I was the first to go to school, the first to travel on the bus, the first to visit Paris on a school trip. Sometimes this positioning gave me courage, sometimes intense shyness.

Shyness because after the age of nine I warp-sped into something tall and gangly. At the top of my tall body, over structurally necessary big feet, I grew a determined fringe which *had* to touch my eyelashes; absolutely no shorter. Hair is an excellent camouflage while growing up in the body of a beanpole.

At sixteen I changed schools and began to board away from home. That was good. It stretched me out. They thought I might be really quite bright from what they could see under all that hair. The teachers thought I should aim for Oxford or Cambridge – it could be the road to something.

But first there would be The Exams. Now that the possibility that I might achieve something exceptional had appeared, these A-level exams rose up before me, filling the horizon with scribbles and scribbles as far as the eye could see. It was always going to be a question of bullseye or complete failure. It was touch and go, and I am sure Mum gained a few grey hairs over the two weeks of peaks and troughs and occasional emergency trips back home to Calm Me Down.

But it worked. Luckily I conquered the nerves, got A grades and was offered a place at Cambridge without the need to take the usual Oxbridge exams.

No one turns down such an offer so, at the end of summer 1985, I set off for Selwyn College, Cambridge. I carefully packed up all my records in boxes with little catch closures. The Doors, Led Zeppelin and the recently discovered Bob Marley all came with me before The Smiths and the *Rocky Horror Picture Show* turned up. Bob's album cover had a saffron-yellow background with large red letters. Inside he was telling me to open my eyes and to look within. Advising me with a gentle swell to ask myself if I was satisfied with the life I was living. I didn't know yet. It seemed far too early to be sure or even ask such questions.

First I had to enter the world of Cambridge, which was far away from the Whitstable I knew, a seaside town where elderly ladies carefully put their daily shopping in wheeled trolleys then pull them along behind them on their walk back home. Their faces were lined by the strong winds blowing off the shore and a life lived through at least one world war. I was leaving all of this now. I was off to posh, posh Cambridge where anything was possible.

CHAPTER 7

THE HOPES

'Where *is* your mother?'

Dad was tapping his fingers on the steering wheel of the estate car parked in the driveway. I was in the back, in a long grey skirt which moved like tissue paper in the wind. My hair was long and dark blonde. We were off to Cambridge. My trunk and music were in the boot. Lucy and Toby were old enough to stay at home.

I didn't say anything in reply. Dad was always early and Mum was always late. That was a total certainty in our family.

Across the garden came Mum, huffling and buffling, sucking her heels out of the grass. Her navy-blue smartness was mixed with a few grey dog hairs.

She opened the passenger door. 'Sorry, darling, I just realised I needed to leave the dog food out and put that load of towels in the washing machine.' She sat down, put the seat belt across. 'Right, well, I'm here now.'

Dad swallowed a mutter and looked in the rear-view mirror. I smiled back.

'OK, Ems, let's go.' Dad learnt to drive on tanks when he did his National Service. Enough said. Off we went.

After a while Dad checked in with me. 'How are you feeling back there? Excited?'

'Yeah, yeah, I'm OK.'

I didn't want to say I was nervous and not sure how this whole Cambridge thing would be. I loved my home but obviously I needed to grow up. I had been to Cambridge once before, for my interview. This time I had luggage with me, and my parents.

Cambridge is in the middle of flat land about two hours from Whitstable. It is impossibly beautiful in places, the buildings imagined by the most tasteful princess elegantly looking out from a perfect spire. It has functioned as a university town for centuries and you can feel it as you pass by the ancient buildings which have housed generation upon generation of big brains.

I am sure that before David got up the courage to face Goliath he must have swallowed a little and felt some shyness, standing in his giant shadow. Approaching Cambridge was a little like this.

We arrived at Selwyn College, which was a mixture of ivy growing up beautiful brick buildings and a modern residence called Cripps Court. This was where I would live for my first year; across the road from the Porters Lodge and the perfect grass of the college's quadrangle.

I had one eye on other students as they wandered past; saying hi, checking out their clothes; looking for signs of compatibility.

Mum was keen to see my room in J block and the nearby kitchen. She opened the fridge and checked the view from the window. We wedged my burgundy bike into one of the metal bike slots by the entrance. OK, I had clothes, music and a bike. I was as ready as I was ever going to be. Now I needed Mum and Dad to go because it just wasn't cool to hang out with your parents.

'So proud of you, Em,' he said on leaving, giving me a dad hug.

I waved them off on Grange Road and walked back to my little room and put out my records, standing them up in their wire stands. It was all quiet and new and I was not quite sure what to do next.

Cambridge was definitely a big step; further away from Whitstable, our family dog and my yellow bedroom. In the final two years of my schooling, while boarding, I had gone home a lot at weekends; the school had been about an hour from home and Mum had been happy to pick me up and drop me back if I asked. Now I would be on my own for eight intense weeks of essay crises and fitting in.

I knew a couple of people from school who had come to other colleges at Cambridge: Richard at Queens and Louise at Girton. Besides them, I would just have to dive in here and find new friends.

There were eight of us in my year at my college for English and they would be my main peer group for my first year. Juliet was small and very pretty, from Wales; Catherine was from Bristol and had a good grasp of political issues like nuclear stuff and women's rights. We went to parties together. Juliet lent me her multicoloured leggings which glowed fluorescent in the dark.

Over the months we all changed together, forming clearer ideas and looks to explain who we were. For me that meant not wearing shoes, reading a lot of Imagist poetry and hanging out at the university theatre, building stage sets for the weekly productions. I put postcards of famous paintings on my bedroom walls and took to cutting hair as a sideline. I bought some black boots with spiky heels and accidentally stepped on the shiny black disc of 'Panic' by The Smiths left on the floor; an EP with a piercing.

Underneath all the changes, I wished I had a clearer, definite *thing*. But I didn't. I was quite interested in knowing about English literature but not *quite* enough. I wanted friends but still preferred lying on my own in the long grass daydreaming. I wanted a boyfriend but was alarmed by the noises and movements it involved when the potential candidates got excited.

A big part of me missed being back at home, where life was easy and less was expected of me. Maybe I was just too young to know how to hold all these balls in the air at once without wanting to cry. A Buddhist might call it a sense of dukha, of floating discontent.

I used my bike (to which I had soldered cow bells so it made a warning noise as I cycled) to dash from this to that like a district nurse, turning up, but never staying too long in one place.

During my first year at Cambridge my parents moved to America with my dad's job. Friends of Mum's lived in our house in Whitstable which felt a little odd as I had lost my Plan B bolthole. I carried on at Selwyn, staying up late listening to Otis Redding's 'Sittin' on the Dock of the Bay' with Rob in the year above. Listening to it, I realised I too was ready to let letters drop off and move on.

Underneath all the activity I began to want to be somewhere else. The unsettled feeling was strengthening into a desire to actually leave. After the first year of studying English, I switched to History. It was a compromise decision, based on a discussion with my parents, who were keen for me to stay at Cambridge. They felt a change of subject would improve things and help me settle.

The history course was interesting, especially learning about the English Civil War. During that era many odd little groups were set up in response to political and religious change in England. They were called 'dissenters'. I liked this word. They later became known as 'Nonconformists'. I liked this word too. There were the Diggers, the Enthusiasts and the Seekers as well as the better-known Levellers and Puritans. All of them were Christians who had separated from the Church of England and campaigned for its reform.

It was inspiring to learn about people creating ideals to live by and I had a wonderful tutor in John Morrill, but despite these high points and my interest in the subject, my happiness seemed lost and my day-to-day discontent all too real.

In the autumn of my third year, I rested wearily against the side wall of the college's payphone and took a deep breath. I called Mum and Dad in America and got it out: the thing that had been sticking in my throat like a prickly fishbone.

'Mum, I've left.'

'What?'

'I've left, Mum,' I repeated. 'I've told John Morrill.'

There was silence down the phone, coming from thousands of miles away.

Another 50p. *Clunk.* The phone was eating it up.

'I can't do it any more,' I added for emphasis, filling in the silence.

'Oh, Emma, really.' She sounded exasperated.

I knew Dad would be gutted.

'Sorry, Mum. I am *really* sorry. Honest.' I felt such a bloody failure.

Beep beep beep. My money had run out.

I knew I had let them down. I knew they would be disappointed. But it was done now and there was no going back.

I left quietly. As I had changed to History, I was seeing less of Juliet and Catherine by then. I said goodbye to them but did not go into detail as to why I *had* to go. I don't find it easy to say how I feel, even now, and all students know that the late teens–early twenties bridge is a hard one to walk *and* talk on. They knew I had lost the glow of the fluorescent leggings. It was obvious I had to find some sparkle from somewhere else.

I left my mark on the place: a plaque outside the university library stating that '*Shoes must be worn on entering the library.*' It was put up in my honour after a librarian in an orange-checked skirt peered under the table at my bare toes and asked me to leave.

I went to be with Mum, Dad, Lucy and Toby in our new home in Summit, New Jersey. From a huge, white, weather-boarded house with a veranda my dad was commuting into Lower Manhattan each day. Things were a little tense as there was a fair amount of family confusion flying about. The move to America had not been without its stresses. Dad still wanted an Enid Blyton life and lots of picnics. Mum was trying hard to adapt to American life in which everyone kept wishing her a 'good day' – this was driving her crazy. Lucy had dyed her hair dark blue; Toby had grown a pink Mohican. We weren't exactly helping them to blend in.

Perhaps to join in with the confusion, or to make a silent protest, or to try to feel more how I really wanted to feel, I decided to cut off all my hair. I got some hair clippers from the mall and took some time to move them round my head, learning I needed to fold my ears down to get round the edges neatly. There – I now had no hair and my head felt light and something about this new state felt very right to me, essential to the new start I was looking for. It may have looked odd to others though; like the actions of a disgruntled twenty-year-old.

Dad said, 'Oh, Ems, your hair. You had such lovely hair,' as I walked down the pale, carpeted stairs from the bathroom for the first time. But I felt relieved not to have the hassle of shampoo, conditioner, drying hair and picking off split ends in moments of boredom. The simplicity of it was so wonderful.

Hair though was so much simpler than educational decisions. I couldn't stay on indefinitely in America with my parents. What exactly would I do there? Besides, having taken one foot out of the family and the family house, I didn't want to end up with both feet back there.

I spent a few weeks doing artwork on the floor of our garage before returning to Cambridge hoping I could study art.

To earn money I got a job in an Iceland supermarket in Cambridge, complete with a red-and-white-checked uniform. I sat at a till and pressed numbers on buttons in the days before scanners made those bleeps. They asked me to wear a wig which was itchy and tended to slip forwards as I leant to press the buttons. It was not satisfactory.

I got a place on a year-long Art Foundation course at Cambridge Art College. Once on the course I stopped the job, burned the wig and concentrated on my studies.

I enjoyed the course. I got the chance to set light to things and use a lot of masking tape. It was like remaining a child for a little while longer. Paper and charcoal; making simple lines on white paper. It was a strange alchemy which gave me more confidence that I could connect to something and find a feeling of joy. Here some sparkles lived; some stars began to reappear in the sky.

At the end of the course we were given the chance to do our Final Show in the grounds of the Astronomy Centre on the outskirts of Cambridge. It was a large area with a white, domed structure in which there was an enormous, rotating telescope. This telescope looks at stars and then plots them as numbers on huge pieces of paper; drawing sky maps with a night eye.

I decided to do something directly at the site rather than bring artwork along to display there. I asked permission to dig down into the land in a lightly wooded area just to the side of the green lawns and away from the clever dome.

Permission granted, I cycled back and forth every day from my shared student house to the site, kitted out in shorts with cigarettes shoved in my back pocket and a shaven head. Hey, I was young and a student – it was not so odd a look! I set out an area about eight foot long by four foot wide and started to dig. It was a simple task that just needed determination, a bit like knitting. I left the spade there each night, as it was too tricky to carry back and forth on the bike. Day after day, I dug, smelling earth and watching the layers of mud and shingle revealing themselves; a Battenberg of earth and shells and worm tracks. The sound of the spade cutting, its metal edge slicing through the ground, became my companion. To one side of the hole a large mound of earth was forming a clumsy pyramid.

As I dug further down I had to stand in the hole, throwing the earth off the spade, behind my shoulder and over the edge. Eventually I had to use a bucket and a ladder to take the earth out. Going up and down on the ladder with full buckets was tiring. I can't believe I managed to do it, unfit smoker as I was at this point. I think this unlikely physical strength came from a mental determination which directly drove my muscles.

Deeper down a tree root revealed itself coming out from one of the end walls. It wiggled out into the space before turning downward, entering the floor of the pit. People had started to call it 'the pit' now. It wasn't a name I wanted but it was hard to find the right name for whatever this thing was.

At around ten feet down I began to worry about the sides collapsing in and decided to stop. It was deep enough. When I stood in it there was definite distance above the top of my head and without the ladder there was no easy way to get out. So once you were in there it was a comfortable space of emptied-out earth with an old tree root running through it. I tried to guess which tree it was connected to in the area around the pit but it was impossible to work out. Seeing deeply buried roots, it can be hard to spot which tree they connect to on the surface of the forest. Now I know this.

When you were inside the pit with the root winding away above your head you could sit or lie down. It gave you an earth-framed view of the sky above. Looking at the blue and the clouds passing from this point of view was a concentrated experience which made people become quiet and reflective. As if they were seeing the essence of sky for the first time. Or feeling a freedom that can only be understood through confinement.

I liked being in there although there was an element of risk attached. To get into the pit it was best to go down a long metal ladder which was then lifted up. This meant you could be in there by yourself but it was reassuring to have someone at the top as they could drop the ladder back down for you when you called out.

For the first time I had a feeling of something being right. It was just a little disconcerting to notice that it wasn't quite what I had thought 'right' might look like.

If I had been more confident the walls were not going to cave in I might have been braver; stayed longer, even slept in it, but the fear of being accidentally buried by earth led me to proceed with caution.

After the art show I had to fill in the pit for fear of someone or some animal falling into it. It was very simple to pile the earth back although it didn't fit in very well, leaving a prehistoric-looking mound arching out of the ground in the area between the trees. I thought it might settle back down in time like biscuits in a tin.

Approaching the end of the foundation course, I took my portfolio of life drawings, photos and expressionistic self-portraits to an interview at Goldsmiths College, London, and was lucky enough to be offered a place. Goldsmiths College had a top-notch reputation as a place to study Art. Damien Hirst was a recent alumnus and was making waves; there was a buzz about the place and what might come out of it.

South London was a huge contrast to the beauty of Cambridge with its long lawns and quiet bikes. Now I was in a basement flat with a whiff of damp and strangely boarded-up shop fronts outside. It had taken a while before I could find any insurance company to give me contents insurance. Doing a BA in Fine Art made up for all of that, and the relaxed – some might say downright chaotic – nature of South London was easy to blend into.

Goldsmiths gave each of its Fine Art students their own space in which to make stuff, like having a room of your own. In addition there were intelligent tutors to guide students, usually through debate rather than instruction. It was a wonderful combination of structure and freedom. Goldsmiths was well known for its cutting-edge 'conceptual' approach to Fine Art, so there was not much traditional drawing and rather more film making and 'installation sculpture'. I made various large sculptural pieces using foam and light projections. My tutorials were often discussions around the human body and its impermanence; my work was usually expressions of these themes.

I dyed my cropped hair bright white using a thick paste. I got black cycling shorts, black tights, retro platform shoes and a loose, luminous, lime-green top. Yes, I was definitely an *art* student.

I thought this might impress Lars. He was the Norwegian art student in the year above who was gluing Formica to the college front doors as part of his final-assignment installation. He gave me some lovely Jackie O sunglasses for helping him, but nothing more.

CHAPTER 8

THE SILENCE

Towards the end of my second year of the three-year course in Fine Art at Goldsmiths, Mum told me that Dad had been diagnosed with lung cancer. They had taken time to digest the information before telling us. I was in London and they were back living in the family home in Whitstable so I wasn't in the hub of things. It was hard managing coursework in one place while your heart was in another. I dyed my hair back to its original light brown colour and began to grow the length out.

Before Dad fell ill I hadn't paid attention to the dynamics of their marriage. We were just a family and often one pulling in different directions, our dogs forming the centre point which we all came back to. The illness drew Mum and Dad together in a new way; attending appointments, discussing details. They were clearly a team focused on a very real task. Lots of stuff which they talked about before or Mum got huffy about and Dad got quiet over didn't crop up any more.

Mum wanted to have an idea of a realistic time frame. Dad began to organise things, using his office skills to prepare a folder called 'Project Hope Not'. He moved money around to 'protect' us and Mum. He organised a lot of quick building work to be done on the house, probably doing stuff he had put off for years. He was tidying things up.

He hadn't long retired. He and Mum had planned to travel, perhaps to South America or Tibet, but now they were going back and forth to the Chaucer Hospital in Canterbury, and waiting.

The initial treatment in late 1991 and early 1992 was successful. However, in late summer 1992, the cancer returned, entering his brain in the form of tumours. There was talk of 'primaries' and 'secondaries' as the growth of this cancer took on its own biography. Although we could not see it, this thing had been quietly multiplying and was now clutching on everywhere inside my dad.

After Christmas 1992 he became very tired. He sank deeper into the sofa as it grew larger than him. It became an effort for him to put his slippers on. He did not want to go into hospital so we moved a bed into the downstairs playroom for him.

Then we watched the slow process of Dad shrinking away. My sister and I smoked a few joints up in our attic rooms throughout this time. It helped us to numb the pain of the fact that We Could Do Nothing to stop what was happening downstairs. The cancer turned us all into bystanders. Lucy and I stood and sat and leant with our eyes red, either from crying or being zoned out.

Dad didn't talk about the situation. Just the one time, on the sofa, with the TV on, he said, 'I feel awful leaving you kids like this.'

That was about it. That was all he said and it was sort of to the ceiling, not to us directly. I was twenty-six, Lucy twenty-four and Toby twenty-two, but we were still his 'kids'. He just got on with it, with 'leaving', and we followed his lead. I never talked to him about what it felt like to know, with such absolute certainty, that he was dying. I never asked him if he was afraid to die. We comforted him with food in different forms and, eventually, helped to turn his body to ease the discomfort of long periods of time lying on sore parts of his body. We listened to his strange conversations which became influenced by the brain tumours and the morphine. It was unnerving when Dad was talking like he was no longer Dad.

I spent a lot of time upstairs in my yellow attic room doing three-thousand-piece puzzles on my wooden floorboards. They were mainly of historical scenes or pictures of famous paintings; details make puzzles easier.

I listened to Edwin Starr's song 'War' a lot, which asked 'what is it good for' with a simple truth: '... absolutely nothing'. I liked how defiant it sounded. I sang along with it, as loud as I could, until its certainty filled my whole head.

Close to what became the end, Dad reached out to me. I was sitting by him on a small, wooden chair. He made as if to wipe my forehead with his hand. It was a gesture like air passing over dust. As he did this he said, 'I love you.'

These simple words were a moment of lucidity in the midst of what were otherwise morphine- and brain-tumour-induced mumblings. As a family we were not very verbally expressive and certainly the L word was not bandied around; the assumption being we just knew we were loved. To hear him say this before he left was like someone catching you as you fall in terror. It steadied me and gave me a safe place to return to.

On 3 March 1993, as we sat down to eat our lunch, Dad died. Mum called us into the room. She was sobbing.

I held his hand but it made no difference. I had wanted to lie down next to him and stay with him. He was lying on his back, not on his right side. Even so, I thought I could curl up into his little body and go right back to the beginning. His body was collected, promptly, by undertakers who zipped him up in a long black bag and carried him down the concrete path he had walked up so many times.

Even though we had known that he was going to die it was still a shock. Actually being without him was still hard to come to terms with. I suppose no amount of knowing can prepare you for the emptiness of loss.

There were a lot of practical things to do afterwards, which was useful, really, as the pain of losing him was overwhelming. I think if there had not been anything to do we would have all crawled into bed and stayed there, unable to face the daylight. Seeing the sun still able to shine and the grass still able to grow was hard to accept.

At his burial a few days later Mum thought she saw him standing slightly turned as if to watch his own funeral. She said he was standing near the long, black car. I didn't see him but I am pleased she did. I was looking downwards, into the sides of the dugout earth. My heels got stuck in the March mud. I threw a penny-farthing I had been saving down on to the coffin lid for luck. Just in case. Its sound was light and metallic before the heavy earth which went on next.

'We commit his body to the ground, earth to earth, ashes to ashes, dust to dust.'

He was in the earth now and life would take a different course for all of us from here.

We all needed to carry on, each of us dealing with the grief in our own way. It was something that was hard to do together, even though we had so much to share. If we leant against each other we might crack the next one and then we would all fall down, broken.

I became non-verbal and nocturnal. I gulped down the sadness, into my insides. It took a long while for it to dilute and stop clinging like a lump in my tummy. Mum cried a lot, particularly while doing the ironing. I can see now that she had lost the love of her life.

From being back home in Whitstable I returned to London in late spring in order to do my final degree show at Goldsmiths. This was necessary if I was to complete the degree. I wasn't going to *not* finish two degrees and make it look like a habit. Luckily my sister, Lucy, came up to London to help me. Before Dad died she had been engaged and had a sales job in publishing but she had taken a break from both of these.

For the final show all the studio spaces in the Fine Art area were tidied up and each student was given an area in which to make their final piece of work which would be used to determine their class of degree. I had a good space – light with stylish sash windows and one long wall of bricks painted white. The room was effectively divided into two with an invisible line. I shared it with Jason who was a painter. He used black paint to create huge circles on his canvas which he then ran windscreen wipers through to make big liquorice allsorts. His work did indeed look tasty and I believe he went on to be quite successful.

Things were not quite so jolly in my half. It was soon after Dad's death and I could not think of making anything which did not address this huge fact. I decided to construct a standing pillar out of yellow, London bricks. These bricks were stacked on top of each other, two-foot square. I alternated the direction of bricks in the way a child learns with building blocks, an easy way to make a structure stronger. The pillar stood up to chest height. On the top I placed a thin, white, melamine top. On top of that I laid a rectangular metal plate embossed with the words describing the ten key tasks we did when Dad died. It looked a little like all the lists Mum had used as we grew up, except this one was solid. If you worked your fingers into the shapes you could feel the letters rising up from the metal like a language of touch.

Set into the brick wall behind the pillar (that was behind you if you were reading the plate on the white top of the pillar) was a two-foot square of dark purple leather. The leather was tightly held in place by grooves cut into the wall with an angle grinder. The leather was pulled taut into the wall, picking up every underlying detail of the brick. Close up it was like a rubbing left on stretched skin but from further back it became a floating purple square. As evening fell it rested there like a thundercloud left hanging in an empty sky.

I got a first-class honours degree but I had nothing left to say or make or paint. Death does that. Seeing Dad's body dead, his mouth slightly open, a little liquid coming out and dribbling to a stop, does that.

I returned to the family home in Whitstable and got a job in the local old peoples' home just up the hill from the house. I had to do something and I did not want to revert to being a child again, asking Mum for pocket money.

Most of the other carers were older than me and had been doing it for years. I was an oddity but that was OK. I could relax with being odd.

It was the first time I had spent time around truly elderly people. My dad was sixty-two when he died and had not had time to adopt the mannerisms and twinkly eyes a grandfather is thought to have.

Caring for these people, particularly on the night shifts, was about caring for the basic needs of human beings. Physical human existence could look quite depressing in the end. Bodies became wrinkled which was especially strange when the old skin was tattooed. Tattoos and names of loved ones became compressed on skin transparent like tissue paper.

In the old people's home it largely came down to what was still physically possible for those living there. Their bodies had become defined by their weight and volume and the resultant degree of complexity in getting them to a hoist or on to a commode. As carers we had to think of these things and practise patience. These people were working at a speed other than our own. The smell of the place was strongly chemical; it was as if only such a strong dosage would drown out the smell of bodies failing.

After a few months working and not doing a lot else, the out-of-placeness no longer felt comfortable. Slowly I felt the wish to stop hiding and to re-enter the world. I was beginning to let go of the grief.

CHAPTER 9

THE AFTERWARDS

But everything seemed to come crashing down yet again. I had to wonder, was I just highly strung or simply inadequate? A drama queen making too much of a small incident or just Miss Unlucky with the T-shirt to prove it?

Of course I knew logically that the fact that Jakarta had happened was not my fault but it was hard not to feel that somehow the effects of Jakarta *were*, both for me and for him.

After all *I* had survived, hadn't I? I was all too aware that the man might not have. *He* may have died, shot up by all those bullets which left that wall of blood. The alternative would have been incarceration in an Indonesian jail which, if anything, sounded worse. Either way it made me the lucky one, so why was I struggling now? Why couldn't I just go on when I had the chance?

These were dark days and lonely nights.

The lack of a safe space anywhere was so tiring, and I came close to slamming my car into a wall with the exhaustion of it all. Suzi Quatro's 'Devil Gate Drive' invited me to shout loudly inside the car, goading me again and again to come alive, but no matter how much anger there was or passion or fear or miles on the speedometer I just didn't know how to.

I drove to our family's holiday home, a cottage in Somerset, thinking that if I went fast, it would silence the feelings, or if I went to a different place, things would go away. Or if I played the music really, really loud nothing would hurt any more.

Before Somerset I had a series of medical assessments. From these the doctors determined that I had 'complex PTSD', a form of PTSD often associated with entrapment in which there is no clear escape and which results in a loss of identity and sense of self. It can arise most strongly in those who have experienced other forms of trauma prior to a life-threatening event. I didn't have the capacity to research the meaning then but it sounds spot on to me in hindsight. With that diagnosis I learnt I was booked on to the March intensive PTSD residential recovery programme and I returned from Somerset full of hope that real help was in sight.

The course was held in a large Victorian building in the Sussex countryside. Our group of four were all dealing with a situation which had caused PTSD. The course gave each of us time to talk through our experiences, allowing us to fully integrate them into the present. You might think it would be traumatising to talk it all through again but it was so helpful. It took the experience-flashbacks out of the realm of shadows and gave them a sense of a beginning, middle and end. It was a relief to be able to speak about it fully, without embarrassment or the feeling of shame which had lingered in my mind.

The flashbacks and their physical responses decreased and, after an intense week, I left the course knowing I would be able to continue my life; the heavy horizon line had been lifted so I could see and think a little further forwards.

But now what?

I had survived, hadn't I? Survived Dad's death, survived Jakarta, survived PTSD. It seemed I was being given the gift of a second chance, but was it best to fill it with shoes and spreadsheets once more?

In May 1998 I began a phased return to work, under medical supervision, to work in my bank's London office, commuting from Kent. First I worked on emerging debt in Eastern Europe, a new area for me, then on several high-status projects for the CEO, including Y2K, the dreaded Millennium bug. Neither of these new roles exactly satisfied my desire for a more meaningful life.

I spent time back at my home in Faversham walking and doing simple things and wondering what was most important to me. I got a career-change book – something about a parachute, with a brightly coloured cover. It advised people seeking a career change to list the things they like to do best and turn them into a career. Right, so: walking, finding fossils on the beach, being quiet, swimming. It was hard to see how those would pay off a mortgage. *Blast*. Nothing that was important to me actually seemed that useful for standing on one's feet and surviving. *Hmm*.

I *could* go back and truly recommit to the City, but I couldn't. I could go forwards, but there was nothing there yet. I was in a between-a-rock-and-a-hard-place situation, but there was nothing else for it – I had to jump into the unknown. It was a question of making it happen.

On a Friday in June 1998 I resigned. It was all very amicable. The bank threw me a leaving do, a gathering with colleagues on a sunny evening to drink wine and say goodbye. It was a beautiful summer evening in London and, from the balcony, I could see the tarmac of the City sprawling out below. It was being crossed by fast Friday feet. People were rushing for their trains, keen to get home for the weekend.

I felt their speed but I did not need to run any more. I walked into the future at my own pace with no clue of what might happen next.

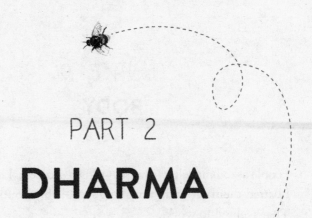

PART 2

DHARMA

CHAPTER 10

BODY

People asked me what I was planning to do next. I had no idea. I batted them off with 'travelling – probably South America'. That seemed to work.

When you give yourself some time to see what might turn up it's tempting to fill that time with plans, especially so you can answer *that* question when people inevitably ask it. I wanted to keep emptying out, not stuffing things back in. I sold my house in Faversham to free myself from a specific location and from the mortgage which tied me to a job. This meant that my mum put up with boxes of stuff in her downstairs dining room as I just stopped and waited, back home again.

Mum loves to flick through brochures and circle ideas in newspapers. This time she spotted an alternative-style holiday in Greece where you could do various courses. One titled 'How to Make Mosaics' caught her attention. I had always loved mosaics and, as there had been no lightning-bolt revelations yet, it seemed like a good idea.

I studied the front of the brochure – lots of smiling, good-looking thirty-somethings were grouped in stripy T-shirts with their chins thrown back, ready to take a bite out of the blue, blue sky. The unspoken strapline was: *Come here and find your Mr Right*. Perhaps there was more to Mum's plan than met the eye.

Up to this point you might have noticed (as my mum had) that relationships had not been a huge part of my life. A lack of physical confidence and a slight fear of physical intimacy – I was still in the generation when the fear of getting pregnant by accident was enough of a contraception in itself – meant I had spent more time in my brains than my loins. I had had a relationship in London with Bill (he of the watch), which had been good but it ended just before I left for Hong Kong.

At this point, and even despite the entrails of Jakarta, I still really did *want* to fall in love. I longed for the happiness and the feeling of being cherished which would come in a relationship. I was sure it would offer the best way to finally feel at peace. I was sure because, well, that's what I had read and watched and listened to and just assumed was right. And so, now, yes, it was time for *love* and Greece might just be the right place to find it.

So with nerves in one hand and sun cream in the other, I set off for Greece. From Athens airport I had to take a long ferry journey east. I watched from the back of the boat as it churned up seawater, throwing it over like a French plait. The whole journey to the island of Skyros took quite some time and a fair bit of exchange of 'you OK?' with green-tinged strangers but it was worth it. We arrived at a brilliant coastal bay studded with houses built of rounded stones set amidst trees, their bark bleached grey by the sun. The hours of travel were dumped as fast as my luggage hit the ground. *Greece, I'm ready for you!*

Later I sat down with some white wine and a straw, looking out across the bay, lapping up the hot, dry Greek summer. I was one of thirty or so assorted adults open to see what was in store. We were rounded up and given our intros before signing up for our chosen courses. I went with the plan and signed up for the mosaic-making, a drama thing and morning meditation.

Around us were glorious smells of cooking mixing with sun oil being spread on skin left bare around the thin straps of summer tops and colourful swimsuits. Everyone was ready to get into Greece and enthusiastically exchanging smiles and details with their new companions.

Lunch was outside under sunlit tables, with big bowls of rough-cut vegetables, pasta and delicious breads and olives. I chatted to my neighbours over lunch: Jacquie was a social worker about my age and in need of a break from the frontline; Debbie was a keen writer here to do the creative-writing course with a well-known poet. There seemed to be a lot more women than men around, and I wondered if it might be wiser to concentrate on catching a tan rather than anything else.

Initially keen to produce a masterpiece on the course, I soon realised that mosaics for beginners was a fairly crude activity involving a lot of glue and sticky gaps. *Hmm.* I held up my whale, which promptly dropped its tail on to the floor, becoming an aubergine at sea.

Perhaps mosaics were not going to offer me the path I was searching for.

After a bracing swim the next day, I gave the mosaics a miss and lolled on a chair in the sun in the communal area enjoying having nothing to do. In the circular area above the dining tables I noticed a woman doing something which looked rather beautiful. Was it jumping, gymnastics or karate? Either way it looked intriguing, with a clear, physical flow which reminded me of painting while also looking inwards with a quiet sense of absorbed concentration. Somehow it reminded me of looking up at the sky from deep within the earth.

I asked one of the staff who walked by with a large tray of couscous. It turned out to be yoga and it was being done – if that was the right verb – by the course teacher. Sharon was apparently brushing up on near perfection before teaching her class that afternoon. I had the time so, after lunch, I put on a fitted purple top and cropped leggings and decided to give it a go.

It turned out I was a natural. Can you believe it? I reckoned running down the corridors in Jakarta had given my hamstrings extra stretch. I turned out to be a super-flexi shape maker. And I loved it. I *loved* it.

Forget angels singing and harps playing – I was feeling my legs, my feet, the arch of my back, and with them I could take up space in different ways. I was in shock, it was so good. I was made of rubber. You just had to show me the shape and I was there. No one was more surprised than me. At school I was rubbish at sport, somewhere between a daddy-long-legs and a giraffe. My parents were even called into my school when I was a teenager when concerns were raised that I might have some kind of disability, such was my propensity for falling off wooden things in the gym.

Now, for the first time in my life, I was enjoying having a body and seeing what it could do. Crossing things over, under and through, I lunged, backbent, held my toes and lengthened my neck. I felt like fleshy origami thriving on sunshine and feta cheese.

I had found *my thing*. Here it was, at long last: my actual thing. I could have tattooed a big arrow next to my grin saying, *Yoga Did This*, with Fred Flintstone in the background cheering 'yabadabadoo'.

Mosaics was history, yoga was the future and, after a few more sessions, Sharon asked if I could do the 'lotus' pose, demonstrating it herself as I did not know what she meant. Lotus is a classical sitting position in yoga, typically used in meditation. Its Sanskrit name is Padmasana: 'padma' meaning 'lotus flower', and 'asana' meaning 'seat' or 'posture'. If you look at pictures or statues of the Buddha or yogis meditating you will see this position; the left leg folded in first, heel high up on the right thigh and then the right leg folded to lie on top of the left thigh. In this balanced crossover the soles of the feet lie flat and upward-facing.

Luckily I was able to whip straight into this posture and, as I did, I immediately felt an enormous surge of energy at the very base of my spine, slightly underneath me as if my heels had pressed some unseen button. I experienced the feeling of coming home to something perfectly right. What a strange thing, that a particular arrangement of one's lower limbs could have such a powerful effect. Clearly yoga was something very amazing and a far cry from a bums, tums and thighs class!

After our practice that day Sharon and I sat and chatted. We had started to do this after classes as the dual effects of the yoga, both calming and energising, settled into our bodies with a happy smile. This time as the sun was setting over a hill she told me I really should continue studying yoga and suggested that I go to Maui in Hawaii to learn from Nancy Gilgoff. I said I would think about it. After we finished I went to sit on the open balcony of the centre's stone building. It was on the first floor, overlooking the rocks and sea below. Various people were relaxing and lounging about on it; we knew each other sufficiently to comfortably share space without too much effort now.

I coloured in a circular mandala which was being drawn by a number of people. The first person draws a circle and then, from the centre of it, draws outwards with various shapes and colours, creating a spontaneous patterning. They then hand it on to the next person, who then adds their bit and so on, passing it on until the circle is completely filled with colour. It was a relaxing thing to do and a long way away from my life of calculating debt/equity ratios. Part of me thought it was all a bit naff, but when you are in a life-pause you can let a bit of naff go.

My hair was long, swept up at the back by a curved silver clip like a fern leaf. I had a low-backed pink top on and my back was brown from the Greek sun. I completed my shapes and passed it on, moving to sit on the ledge of the balcony, closer to the salt smell of the sea.

Suddenly I was aware of sitting in a vertical shaft of freezing cold air. Goosebumps sprung on to my bare skin. I had taken on the shape of a large, winged bird, perched high up on a grey stone building, sitting in a niche looking out from a neck poked forwards. Far below me was a wide, green landscape of trees. I could feel my back was muscular and powerful; my wings were guards at my sides. Around me were the sounds of birds calling out, circling. Their clear sounds filled the whole space.

I had a moment of understanding and it went like this: *You have to go and sit in all the places you have sat before. Then you can begin.*

Yes, really. I'm not kidding.

I sat there in shock.

Where did that come from?

I waited to see if anything else was going to happen but my body warmth returned, complete with the appropriate limbs.

I was completely taken aback by this experience. Nothing like it had ever happened to me before. But I trusted it – partly because it was too weird not to and also because it just felt so true. It gave me some kind of confidence that the right path was beginning to emerge. A confidence I kept inside. I didn't tell anyone, as I had no words to describe something so profoundly felt.

The key thing about this was the complete *certainty*. It had taken some time for it to show up. I had eaten a lot of meals, read a lot of books and gone to a lot of places – even if I had not actually kissed a lot of frogs – before I got this feeling of absolute certainty. Now I knew the direction I needed to head in.

I put the white charger – armoured knight thing on hold.

Back in England, I called International Enquiries for Nancy Gilgoff's number – this was before the find-everything-on-Google era. I called her and she said to come to Maui.

My things were still packed in boxes at my long-suffering mum's.

I went off to find yoga and yoga teachers.

It was a long journey to Hawaii with the sun continually rising as the plane went backwards across time zones. I arrived feeling a little shaky.

At the airport I picked up a burgundy, left-hand drive, automatic car with slightly spongy brakes and gingerly began driving on the other side of the road.

After a good hour going east, I found my accommodation: a wooden 'hut' at the bottom of a long field with a gravel path ending under a big tree. It was rented out from a couple who lived in a long bungalow at the other end of the field. We were like aristocrats, set at either end of a very long table.

The hut was situated in the shade of the tree, with a tiny loo, bed and kitchen area inside. It had a TV that went into banded black-and-white dots and a shower head attached to the outside wall. As this hut-home was at the end of a large field I hoped it was fairly private.

At first, I kept waking up in the middle of the night, startled by a thudding sound. I was slightly alarmed, until I realised it must be the coconuts falling off the tree.

I liked the smallness of the place, its simplicity, and Maui was a wonderful place to study yoga. It was 'pranic', as yoga texts would say. It was full and alive; lush plants, trees, flowers and fruits gave the air an intoxicating quality. Everything looked well fed and content. Even the mosquitoes were laid back, flying far slower than I remembered in other places.

'Prana' was explained to me by Nancy as the yogic word for 'life force', rather like 'chi' as in t'ai chi or chi gong. It seemed you could loosely translate it as meaning 'breathing' but really it was much more than that. It reminded me of light sabres and references to the 'force' being 'with you' when *Star Wars* had come to Whitstable cinema and Dad slept through the battle scene.

Nancy Gilgoff was often a hugely useful source of information. She was a well-known ashtanga yoga teacher who had studied extensively in India and now lived in Hawaii, teaching in a wooden building with prayer flags hanging over the door. She taught a mixture of homegrown students and visitors, such as me, who came for short periods to concentrate on their practice.

Every day I travelled in my car from my hut-home to the yoga building for a practice which started at 8 a.m. and went on for a good couple of hours. Ashtanga is a very physical form of yoga with set sequences described as 'series'. You start with series one, the primary series, and move up as your capacity and teacher see fit. There were about twenty of us practising the postures of the first ashtanga yoga series, set up in two lines with Nancy walking down the middle, calling out the postures and the number of breath counts (one to five) to hold them for. She followed the style of many ashtanga teachers in giving us physical adjustments to your yoga postures, encouraging your spine to lengthen, your seated twist to deepen a little bit further. I really enjoyed this feeling of my body becoming more malleable, less 'held' and watching it change.

After morning practice I would return home for breakfast or, after a while, to have breakfast with Harry who lived in the barn next to the yoga place. Harry had been studying yoga with Nancy for years. He had glasses and a beard and was a musician. It turned out he had been up on charges for drugs at some point in California, had come to Maui and stayed there. I am really not sure what happened to the charges. Harry was a little vague about a lot of things. Over a late breakfast we would eat the kind of food that body-conscious yogis eat; dried and fresh fruits and types of bread which sounded like they could be reused as birdseed.

Harry would sit on his throw-covered sofa and strum his guitar. He had the attributes of island cool: a yogi with vague links to a murky past and an ease with amplifiers. It was nice to have his company, especially if I got a little nervous with the coconuts and the outdoor shower.

My sleep at this stage was better but not always totally Jakarta-free. If no longer a fully fledged flashback, memories of the Polaroid and the slump of the body against the wall would still arise. It was unsettling not to know what had happened to this man. As my fear decreased, the wish to show him kindness grew stronger. A little like a prayer.

I spent around three months in Maui, concentrating on mastering the technical aspects of what you physically do in series one of ashtanga. I could have stayed longer but I decided to keep expanding my yoga knowledge. I just wanted to keep on moving.

I returned briefly to England to apply for another American visa then left for New Mexico in the dry desert of America's Southwest. There was an appealing artistic leaning to Santa Fe and I had heard of a yoga teacher there called Tias Little. Santa Fe had a well-established yoga community where yoga was a daily part of many people's lives so there were plenty of teachers, studios and good bookshops.

I started out in the youth hostel along one of the big roads leading into Santa Fe. The streets were filled with signs, advert boards and places to allow you to do everything you could wish for without getting out of your car. Santa Fe itself was very attractive with older-style, mud-built buildings and historic sites connected to the opening up of the Southwest.

In Santa Fe I had the time to browse the large bookshops and read some of the Buddhist books on offer. I got a set of Buddhist quotation cards, like a set of daily spiritual recipes to follow. I am not sure I understood much or even remembered them particularly, but I liked to have them around and I knew my mind was once again beginning to lean towards the philosophy of serenity I had seen as a child.

I expressed an interest in this Asian philosophy at an early age. My mum's parents had both travelled widely and our Whitstable house contained objects from Burma (now Myanmar), where her father had spent some time. There was a large metal gong and beater, and an intricate mother-of-pearl-inset table. But the object which caught my attention was the Burmese reclining Buddha, set on a golden-painted structure a little like a chaise longue.

His face was what I might, as an adult, call serene. As a child I thought he looked like the happiest person I had ever seen. I knew I wanted this happiness to come close to me.

I asked for the Buddha to be moved into my bedroom. There I positioned him so I could see him as I fell asleep, mirroring his posture in my own bed. The Buddha lay on his right side, his right elbow resting on the support, allowing his right hand to elegantly curl under his head. His left arm rested along the undulations of his side body. His left foot was placed, with neat toes, on top of his right foot. It's the classical position for a reclining Buddha from that area of the world, the position the Buddha lay in as he left his physical body.

While I was travelling the world, this Buddha was in my room at the family home in Whitstable, waiting. He was in the company of the two statues I had brought back with me from Hong Kong, one in my hand luggage and the female nun coming later in the trunk.

I was not clear how yoga and Buddhism connected but I was being drawn to both like a magnet, and both were widely available in Santa Fe.

In the daytime I attended classes with Tias Little, amongst other teachers, and continued my quest to understand yoga. I diligently kept a journal with notes on yoga poses, I learnt their Sanskrit names and I improved my understanding of anatomy. I was beginning to move from wanting to be a practitioner to becoming an accomplished expert! At some point along this journey I probably went from wanting to heal my body and myself to wanting to be good at something. That's fine but, as many people will tell you, when you want to get good at something in the physical-body department it can move you away from acceptance and self-compassion – it can move you away from Yoga with a capital Y. But I was not able to see this so clearly back then.

I made friendships at this time but no real relationships. Perhaps I was having too many chats with yoga friends Heather and Caryn to have time to look for anything else.

At the end of 1999 my US visa was running out and New Mexico was heading into winter. I decided to buy a ticket to Australia and follow the warmth to Byron Bay on the East coast.

Flying from the US to Australia is a significantly shorter route than flying there from England so it seemed a logical idea. Even so, the flight was still long, looking down on endless expanses of water. It made me appreciate that England is only an island by the skin of its teeth. This Australian island was the real deal in definition terms – it was in the middle of a serious amount of water.

I had little knowledge of the southern hemisphere besides a loose awareness of the clichés of beer, kangaroos and a tendency to refer to women as 'sheilas'. I didn't think it boded too well, to be honest, but Australia boasted the accomplished ashtanga teacher Dena Kingsberg. Dena was held in high esteem in the ashtanga world and she lived in Byron Bay on the Gold Coast.

Because ashtanga can be such a physical activity, just imagining it can be tiring. For instance, move up into a handstand, starting with both hands on the ground; come down from the handstand and swing your legs through your arms into the shape of a 'V' to place your bottom on the ground, with your back and outstretched legs upwards in the air, making the two sides of the 'V'. I could never do that particular move but I am sure Dena could. I loved my time in Australia. The skies were wide – something to do with the curvature of the earth – which made the clouds and the sun feel like they were arching and expanding over your head. I was standing under a geographic halo. The country's remoteness gave it the feeling that it had developed along a different, unique trajectory and that felt good. The weight of centuries of European buildings piling up on top of each other was a long way away.

Byron Bay was young and full of people interested in yoga, surfing, crystals and fruit smoothies. I bought a short, pink, cropped top to go with the tight orange jeans I had got in Santa Fe. I was gaining a whole new wardrobe. I had a few strands of my hair braided with ribbons. In Australia it seemed nobody was too old for anything.

Again I stayed at the local youth hostel and hired a bike. Every morning I biked to learn with Dena at her timbered yoga studio. We would practise early in the morning, 6 a.m., when the light was just coming inside through the planks of wood. The classes were similar to those with Nancy on Maui in that I was practising the set sequences of ashtanga, which I had moved a little away from in Santa Fe.

Unlike Nancy, however, Dena did not announce the postures or count out breaths but relied on people knowing the sequence they were on and the practice of remaining in most postures for five breaths. This meant that the morning practice, despite having about thirty people in it, was very quiet besides the sound of feet moving and the sound of breathing.

As the days went by, I noticed a highly competent man doing yoga across the room from me. He had black tattoos of simple fern-like shapes on his arms. On his very fit body it gave him an intriguing, tribal look as he practised his silent moves. I could see he was very serious about his daily practice. I just can't resist people who are highly skilled in their chosen field; I decided to get to know him.

Dave, it turned out, was of Maori descent and had come from New Zealand to study with Dena. He had a broken-down old car and a curiously hairless – from the bits I had seen so far – body. We started to stay behind after class on the outside porch and chat before I got on my bike back to town for breakfast.

As keen yoga practitioners and foreigners with time on our hands, we had a lot in common. We began to hang out together on the beach after class. The beaches were stunning, offering beautiful sand that roasted the skin of your toes. You needed to put a hand up, like a sailor on a boat, to look through the sun haze to the water. There your mind could rest in the huge expanse of sky and sea, broken only by the occasional back arch of a dolphin playing.

Dave and I spent time lolling along these beaches and practising yoga postures on the sand. When you are learning to 'drop back' from standing and go backwards into a back bend – what children call 'the crab' – practising on soft sand is very helpful. Dave was great at it; I was still learning. Relaxed and inspired by the sheer beauty of the place, I started drawing again. I bought a large sketchbook, pencils and chalks, and Dave sat still, watching TV, as I drew his profile. He had a thin nose like a bird. I guess he *was* a Kiwi!

With Dave's help my physical strength and stamina began to match my flexibility. It was lovely to share this passion with a partner and Dave was a rather splendid partner to share it with. All the yoga had changed me and I felt more physically confident and expressive than I had before. Added to which, Dave was easy, funny and extremely fit. Inevitably things hotted up and we began a physical relationship; it was hard not to with the sun warming our limbs and all that heavy breathing in the early-morning yoga class! Looking back I am surprised it did not make me more anxious, given it was my first 'relationship' since Jakarta but Australia felt like the end of the earth, far away from the past.

Out of the combination of relaxed happiness and disciplined practice I made progress with a smile on my face. I mastered putting both legs across my back when leaning forwards on the floor – a form of 'turtle' posture, as I suppose carrying your legs on your back like that creates a kind of shell. One day, on taking this posture into an upright position, my hands on the floor, my legs strapped to my back like a tortoise going on a holiday, I snapped some of the cartilage that runs down the centre of the rib cage. The *pop* reverberated around the studio and people looked up. It's the only injury I have ever had in yoga. I rested for the next ten days as it hurt to sneeze, laugh, or turn over. Resting was not easy when I still wanted to be doing yoga but it gave me the chance to listen to Dave telling me about a book he had got from the teacher on the yoga sutras written by someone called Patanjali.

I had vaguely heard about this text, which I understood to be some kind of pithy writing on yoga. I had picked up a copy in a bookshop in Santa Fe and flicked through it. On the cover was an ancient stone statue of a man in profile with snakes rising up to form a shelter over his head. *Weird*. Also, this paperback contained no pictures of physical yoga postures being (per)formed by happy people in bright clothes. So I put it back on the shelf and did not take much notice. But now, in Australia, lying with Dave under a deep, black sky I listened to him speak these small sentences of yoga. He shared them with me, slowly, as a mother feeds a baby.

'Kumbaka': the Sanskrit word meaning a 'pause in breathing'. He gave the sound to me, after rolling it around his tongue. I lay watching the seawater wash over shells. 'Pratyahara': the word describing the process in yoga where the mind moves inwards, away from external distraction. The long 'aaaaa' stretched out from Dave's mouth and into my ear like a sigh of relief. All of it was foreplay to something else, as yet unseen.

Life continued in its sunny bubble. Back in the yoga studio, with the sweat of bodies moving in the early morning light, I was still set on cracking my bugbear: the headstand. It was the yoga posture I found tough, physically and mentally. Balancing in mid-air with no support and my head on the floor made me feel overly tall. It brought up memories of me as a gawky teenager falling off bars in the gym. Whenever I bent forwards to put the crown of my head on the floor I could feel the openness of my neck exposed and my heart quickening. It seemed there were more memories, from other times. This posture showed me the layers of time stored up in my physical body, the layers packed like within an earthen pit; there they all still were. *Is it best to dig them up or just to let them lie? Which is the wiser path?*

When my three-month Australian visa was close to expiring, I got on the bus out of Byron Bay and left the hot sand, and Dave on it, behind me.

I thought I would go to India next – a logical step, given the heritage of yoga – but at the last minute I decided not to. I had heard tales of tapeworms and could practically feel the sliminess of a worm wriggling out of my mouth to look out and around like a periscope. There was no way I was risking that.

Instead I attended an ashtanga yoga teacher-training course in Costa Rica, with a well-known yogi, David Swenson whom I had already done some workshops with and knew to be a highly respected teacher and friend of Nancy Gilgoff.

I hadn't really seen this type of tropical jungle before – where you nearly fall back over as you look up tree trunks trying to see the very top. The sounds of birds, insects and animals echoed around, clearly stating it was their territory. There were twenty of us staying in a wooden retreat centre, practising and learning to teach yoga on a large wooden deck. These huge trees were close by and from time to time large monkeys would swing past the front of the deck on what looked like large ropes of hair, displaying their armpits. They looked at us and we looked at them. Our flexibility was never going to match theirs!

The two weeks of training were sweaty and intense and probably only possible because I was now very fit. In between sessions I learnt to gently sway on a hammock with the sounds of the jungle behind me. I enjoyed taking the postures apart and practising showing others how to do them although I could not say I had the confidence to teach strangers yet and I was probably still more interested in how I was doing than anyone else to have the mindset of a true teacher. Still it was a start.

Throughout my time travelling ashtanga was definitely the perfect form of yoga for me. It was essential in my own process of healing from the physical vulnerability of Jakarta. I grew strong and upright with the clear shadows of a six pack. My confidence in my body grew and, with it, my sense of trust in the world.

However, ashtanga yoga has a competitive edge to it, particularly with its structuring of sequential series based on ability. This gives fertile ground to seeking perfection and finding contentment only through comparison with others which was always going to be a potential pitfall for me. Memories of the dynamics of financial markets began to waft across the space. Fear and greed; you can find that mindset anywhere, it seemed.

I started to wonder if I was repeating old patterns of thought. I was beginning to excel at something, which then raised the desire to be good enough – which in turn was somehow linked to a question quietly running in the background. *Am I good enough? Good enough for what? To be loved? To be happy? Is that what it was all about?*

Whatever it was, it was powerful because it was still hard not to think with these boom–bust thought patterns. They seemed to crop up again and again, so did that mean they *were* me? That possibility didn't sound great since this roller-coaster mind habit was exhausting. How was I going to get myself out of this hole once and for all? I hoped someone would turn up to show me the way.

CHAPTER 11

MIND

After the lush leaves and swinging, long-armed monkeys of Costa Rica, I had to check my bank balance. I couldn't pretend – it wasn't looking quite as rosy any more – the money generated by the sale of my Faversham house was beginning to run low.

Was it time for a rethink? It was nice to be an uber-flexible, widely travelled yogi but perhaps the nomad era was coming to an end. It had been good to dip my toes into the yoga sutras and the deeper aspects of yoga and they *did* sound interesting but I was not sure how I could actually apply them to my own life – well, not unless I put on a white loincloth, daubed ashes on my forehead and moved to India. I couldn't just end up doing physical yoga ten hours a day or I would start emulating a hamster on a New Age wheel. I had met yogis who had done that and they seemed wired on the inside and strained on the outside.

I felt Jakarta was behind me.

It was probably time to return to being a grown-up.

Let's lose the orange jeans and mooch towards some shoe shops.

I spoke to a couple of City headhunters and they were keen to see me and get me a 'brain job' again. Before finalising any plans though I had made a commitment to attend a yoga workshop with yogi friends which was happening in Austin, Texas. A last hurrah before deciding whether I would definitely return to the City.

In Texas George Bush the Younger was being elected for the first time. I watched it on a TV that was in a dark wooden cabinet in my hotel. I attended the yoga conference and saw my friends Heather and Caryn from Santa Fe. After catching up and swapping yoga chat I travelled on to Houston.

I was still waiting to make a decision about the future. I had left cheerful and elusive voicemails for the headhunters in London to buy me some time.

I wanted to look at some paintings by Mark Rothko, the incredible painter of colour – field, abstract paintings. I figured these particular Rothko paintings in Texas must be good as they had been given their own building, the Rothko chapel.

It turned out this 'chapel' was a rather austere concrete building on a university campus. Walking inside, through a low door, the space then opened up. On large, plain walls huge, dark canvases hung down. These paintings are in blacks, whites and greys with blocks of colour divided by a soft horizon line where one colour bleeds into another with such skill it's hard to know where it all begins to change. You could let his large canvases of colour soak into you, like becoming stroke-less paint yourself. Despite these exquisite canvases Mark Rothko did take his own life, as the guidebook reminds you. So strange to be capable of such beauty and such despair.

On the floor, in front of one of the paintings, was a round, purple meditation cushion looking untouched. I sat down on it, neatly cross-legged, care of my flexible yoga hips. I sat and stayed there a good while. I think a couple of people came through. I just sat quietly, with these paintings. Quiet like the sea coming to rest in the middle of a long night.

After a couple of hours I left the chapel and took a winding walk back to my hotel. I found a big park on the way. It was set with sprinklers and dry stone pathways. It was hot and sunny and men with overalls and name tags were working in the park. As I turned towards the sun, it shone through the peppered lines of water fanning out from the sprinklers. Multiple rainbows arched and shone like a row of peacocks fanning out their tails.

At that moment a strong sense of knowing dropped down into me. I understood a picture of the pattern of life, of how it works again and again. Strands were interwoven like an undulating piece of cloth lying down or the strands of DNA structures standing up. Time continuing, spiralling on, with all things connected. It was clear that we all have the chance to carry forward the wisdom we have gained or to decide not to. We can or we cannot, but it seemed best if we did; then threads in the cloth could reach across, make their connection and not get lost.

It is very hard to explain the combination of feelings and diagrams in my head at this point, as you can see. But by the end of that walk, everything was clear and I knew I was not going back to the City. What I needed to do was to sit down and become deeply quiet. If I did that, everything would work out fine. It was moment of certainty number two and it was as obvious as my nose being bang in the middle of my face. I needed to meditate.

In this pre-iPhone-totally-contactable-at-all-times world, I left a voicemail for the headhunters. Choosing a time when I knew the office was closed, I explained that I had decided to pursue other avenues. I did not want to try to explain my plans to another person.

I returned to the UK, packed up some things and drove to the North Somerset coast. There I set up a meditation-home in our little thatched cottage on Sea Lane, the one I visited after my return from Hong Kong before the PTSD residential.

From the front door you could walk down the lane, turning right after a few minutes and a couple of horses, up through fields to look over the sea. The coast itself had been left clear of any buildings. It was wonderful to see the clear line where the cliff edge ended and dropped down to the water like a clear note. The tide bashed away at the cliffs when it was high. When the sea rolled back the arcs of a wave-cut platform were revealed, like the seats of an abandoned theatre.

Inside the two-feet-thick walls of the cottage I slept in one room and turned the other, a narrow bedroom, into a space for meditation. I used an old art box to carry round basic supplies: incense, candles, matches, inspirational books. At the end of the narrow room I set these down with a cushion. This was my space. Small and narrow. Nothing superfluous. Perfect.

I set up a simple daily life, one based around regular meditation, writing and solitary walks. I meditated for many hours per day. I had had little formal instruction or guidance on what meditation was. I just sat and let myself be. It felt good and quite natural. A deep feeling of resting began to happen inside me. I was able to watch the bubbles gradually settle down. I didn't need to look for a missing piece. It was all here already. I just had to sit down and see it.

I also spent time observing nature during my walks; the trees and clumps of earth seemed miraculous when I took the time to notice. I felt very close to them, temporary living beings sharing this space.

Out of this settling I was able to let other feelings come to the surface. Despite the deep pull towards such a simple life, I was beginning to think with more urgency about the relationships in my life, the idea of a soulmate and the big question *do I want to have children?* I couldn't ignore it. I was thirty-four.

None of those questions was likely to be answered living in a cottage in the middle of nowhere. I decided to pack up and head back home to Whitstable.

CHAPTER 12

HEART

It was January 2001, four years after Jakarta, and I was ready to take a new step forwards. Back in Whitstable I took a rest from yoga and meditation in order to concentrate on getting a permanent nest and an income. I found a house, a 1920s end of terrace in a quiet street in Whitstable close to the sea. It was cheap because it needed work. A lot of work – it needed its innards stripped out. Out it all went: pink and green carpets more dust than pile, wallpaper, bright-red greasy tiles and ornamental stones.

Once the house was pared down to a simple starting place, I happily placed my reclining Buddha in the back bedroom with a mattress on the floor. I painted the room a deep saffron colour. Downstairs on the window ledge I placed my Hong Kong monk and nun close to my large collection of yoga and meditation books. I was ready for my new start.

Getting a job was the next essential. Living in Whitstable was not going to offer the career choices I had been used to before, unless I commuted to London. But I was not going back – I didn't want that life again. I wanted to live differently: more locally, doing some gardening, eating organic. I didn't want to be job-defined. I wanted to find some other, less conformist way to live.

Luckily, being able to touch-type paid off and I got a job in an office in Canterbury with a financial advisory company. It was an administration role so it was very relaxed compared to my previous roles and it gave me exactly what I needed at the time.

The job was not driven by the sense of urgency of my old workplace. The staff took a whole hour for lunch rather than bolting something down at their desk with a phone attached to their ear or muting out the conference call while they munched. People had school runs to do and dentist appointments to make. In my previous work life, anything of that nature was made invisible.

I set about establishing a new life with a new rhythm. Mondays to Fridays I would drive the twenty minutes to Canterbury to work and afterwards drive to Faversham or Whitstable swimming pool to do some lengths. I was not practising yoga but wanted to remain fit and had always found swimming similar to yoga in its calming and rejuvenating effect on my body and mind. At weekends I practised my demolition skills on the new house. I took down an old porch and a collapsing lean-to out back. I stripped woodchip paper from the walls and scraped tile grout off the kitchen walls. I wore blue dungarees and goggles and sent dust flying. Mum helped me drive car loads of oldness to the local dump: smelly carpets, softened window frames, broken tiles and fence panels. I returned the house to a skeletal state. Demolition was the easy bit; it was the rebuilding which demanded care.

In the background, behind the DIY, what I was hoping for was the next chapter and I wanted it to be a chapter of love. Would it finally appear from round the corner?

I had already spotted a man on my regular swims at the Faversham swimming pool. He was a graceful crawler, which was attractive to watch – subtly. He hardly disturbed the water as he swum which was unusual, as male swimmers tend to throw water in your lane as they whoosh past, goggles making them oblivious to their multi-directional wake.

He took it at his own pace. I liked that.

He claims I had spoken to him weeks earlier when I told him he was in the wrong lane. I still maintain that this was all his imagination and that 9/11 was the very first day we ever spoke to each other. How could something so magical happen on such a terrible day? At work we all watched the TV with nothing to say, seeing dense clouds of smoke and bursts of flame shooting out from tall city buildings. It was just all the wrong way up.

Trying to digest it all, I still followed my usual routine of going to the pool in the late afternoon. I was pleased to notice he was also there.

After the swim we ended up across from each other in the three-sided shower area – him in the middle of one wall, me in the middle of the opposite wall. Luckily we were the only people in the shower block at that point.

'Incredible, wasn't it?' I said, referring to the day's news.

He looked rather puzzled and said something enigmatic like, 'Oh, yes, it was OK.' He later explained he had not seen the day's news at that point.

I didn't really hear his answer accurately, if I'm honest, as I had the strongest feeling of my stomach wanting to move towards his stomach, to be joined together along a rope. It was a little distracting given that we were both half dressed.

I said, 'Goodbye' – but I meant 'Hello'.

A couple of days later he was, helpfully, standing in the car park as I left the pool. This was when he gave me his name.

Peter.

Hello, Peter. Seeing you makes me happy.

If you had poked me then tangible streams of happiness would have flooded out of me like a child's drawing, full of rainbows, giggles and pigtails.

A few annoying days of *not* bumping into him passed and then… yes, it was *his* shoulder movement, moving in arcs through the water. There he was again. I delayed entering the pool and, when he turned at the lane end, we smiled, and I got in the water.

Yahooooo.

I did not waste time. I invited him round for food at my half-repaired house. He came in a dark blue van and a green fleece jumper. I was nervous answering the door to him. I wondered if my bum looked sexy as I walked into the sitting room in front of him. He brought wine. I had made simple food: bread, cheese, salad. We ate the food from plates which threw rings of shadows on to the floor in the candlelight. On beanbags we listened to music from a player on the floor. 'Midnight Train to Georgia' was the song. Just like the song, it took us a little time to get through the intro bars. We took our time but eventually – aided by the darkness, the wine and the sense that if we were *still* there after so many hours, we really must want to – we moved close and kissed.

Ahhh. The kiss. The feel of his lips with mine.

It's so tricky to know how exactly a first kiss might happen. Who is going to be the one to move their arm or turn their head inwards? Who is going to lean a little and to which side? Wine helped to smooth it out. Peter came into my house a sculptor and left as my boyfriend.

I literally skipped down the road and my aunt Pam raised her eyebrows as if, in despair, to say, 'Here she goes again, getting carried away.'

I didn't care. When someone grabs your heart, you want them to want you. You want them to not be able to live without you. It is a force. He was the planet and I was his moon.

I found it hard to be without him, which was unusual for me. Normally I had positively *required* separation and space. These were the rules I had written for myself when considering intimacy. But Peter made me feel safe. This was partly because of his physical size and partly because he had a gentle manner. He was a big bloke, a sculptor and woodworker. He was keen to point out, with a mischievous grin, 'My hands are my tools.'

I began to step out from Jakarta's final shadow of fear and my automatic threat response. That was a big thing; it opened up a return to being able to love a man with all my heart. I began to welcome him in. Doing the simplest of things was enough; looking at this other being's face was all I needed to do to be filled with the joy of being alive.

To have him completely stay over and for the two of us to have sex did take time. I believe this was rather frustrating for him but I was not able to fall asleep with someone next to me. It still made me too anxious. I was not sure of what might happen in the dark. After serious cuddling, Peter would have to get up and go back to where he was living, still with his dad – it takes time for sculptors to make money! He said, with a groan, that he left 'with elephant balls' because we hadn't completed having sex. But in the end, I felt safe enough to hit the jackpot and have sex and fall asleep naturally with him beside me. I had found a person I wanted. I could trust him.

We went to visit my friends Heather and Ric, in Santa Fe for the Christmas break. The intensity of spending one-to-one time together with minimal distractions was both challenging and helpful.

On the holiday we learnt to adjust to several things. I discovered that I wanted to enjoy sex more and I got annoyed if I kept paying for everything. He discovered that he liked helping me enjoy sex more. He could see that I was annoyed if I paid for everything but he found it hard not to need my help to pay for things, as he was a sculptor. I could see he was not mean, just of limited means. I got it. We managed to see each other's point of view and carry on – an improvement on before.

Not long after we returned from the States I felt confident enough that we should Get Engaged. I explained to him that I was convinced I needed this next step now. I was scared I was going to lose him so I had to make sure I had him. I can hear how bonkers it all sounds now. Peter worked differently and didn't understand the rush. Truth be told, I didn't understand I *was* rushing.

In hindsight I can see the impact of Jakarta still pulling me into a need for certainty. The forces of fear and greed were at work. I was scared and I was in love. If you can trust you don't need such certainty, you can let a relationship breathe and take on its own form, naturally, over time. But I was still suppressing panic on the inside and, because of this, we did it all the wrong way round: we got engaged and *then* talked about stuff like 'how to get married' and 'where we would live' and 'what would happen if we had a child'.

Peter and I had our discussions on how we imagined our combined future. I wanted a kind of contract with clear goals and job descriptions. I think I thought that was what marriage was.

Peter was unable to give me that because the future is unknown – cue offstage noise of a big light bulb switching on above my head. The more I asked for clarity the more annoyed and trapped I suspect he felt. He became stubborn and refused to be exact about any of it.

I responded by getting more and more panicked that I was facing an overwhelming future where I would earn the money, raise the child and do the housework. I thought I would end up trapped and sort of alone. I bailed and called off the engagement. It was all very impulsive and ill thought out. Peter was understandably hurt, particularly as the engagement had not been his idea in the first place.

Then I panicked. Do you see the theme here?

I texted him endlessly, apologised endlessly. I went to his dad's house and sat in my car outside trying to call him.

I love you. I want you.

Please. Come back to me.

His dad had given me flowers, welcoming me into the family, when we got engaged, so there was no way I was pressing that front doorbell.

I am so sorry.

I said that apology a hundred times, like lines scribbled again and again on the blackboard at school. *I am sorry. I am sorry… Here, look – I'll tattoo it on my arm.*

My stomach was in knots. I was in a total panic at the thought of losing this person. I knew I had messed it up and just wanted us to be back together. I put all the white dress stuff firmly back in a box in my head.

A few weeks later we reunited and, I am happy to say, continued in a relationship for another three years with an on-off switch set to manual. 'On' meant 'I can't go on without you. I will drive to wherever you are to be with you'. 'Off' meant 'I can't stand how weirdly different from me you are, how you lose things all the time, hate planning anything and that comedy consists of taking the piss out of people'.

He had his own 'off' list too.

Round and round we went. Gloria Gaynor, the Queen of Disco, sang the retro songs which made you want to dance with a sequinned top in one hand and a tissue in the other. She was right. I never *could* say goodbye, no.

The strange vibration that pierced me to the core was sex. I adored having sex with him; I craved it. Watch a cat. Watch how it stretches out, turns on to its back, wanting to be stroked under the chin, showing you it needs to be stroked, caressed until it purrs. It was this that kept turning me around and around even as I stomped out after a row about his work or my work or why I wasn't more like *this* or why he wasn't more like *that*. Still – still– I wanted to forget all that and lie down, roll on to my back and purr. Every single time it had to be Peter.

Sex was the good bit – always the good bit– and when you find something that good it's hard to accept there are parts that aren't so good, that don't come so easily. We tried to modify our daily differences, hoping everyday life could become as loving and easy as our sex, but we had different ways of doing things and we both found it hard to respect these differences.

Why? I kept thinking.

One: we were both stubborn.

Two: we had both been hurt. Me by Dad's death and events in Jakarta, and Peter by his parents' split when he was a teenager and a girlfriend who had desperately wanted to get engaged and then broken it off – yup, by me.

When these issues came to the surface, things flipped like a pancake in mid-air from sex-row-sex to row-sex-row. You never knew which side would end up on the plate.

A few months into our wonderful upsy-downsy, in-out relationship, I visited the Tibetan monastery of Samye Ling in Scotland for the first time.

I had heard about Samye Ling from Kay, my roommate on a 2002 yoga retreat in Oxfordshire where I was taught breathing practices called chakra pranayama. I had started practising yoga again with a local teacher in Canterbury and was seeking to deepen my understanding with more specialist retreats such as these. This time the practices involved disciplined breathing and visualisations at the seven key points in yoga, the chakras (wheels), which are described as energy centres. There are understood to be six such points in the human body, located at the back of the physical body, set in from the spine. The final point is at the crown of the head.

The lady sitting next to me on the retreat was older than me and seemed very comfortable sitting for long periods of time. Kay was a Buddhist. She spoke to me about the importance of what you do after you have done all these clearing breathing practices. She said it was important to channel these benefits into a meditation practice. I was intrigued, especially as I was fairly sure I didn't actually know how to do that.

Kay recommended I visit the Scottish monastery she often went to and said I should try to get a one-to-one chat with her teacher there, a Tibetan called Lama Yeshe who had done many years in meditation and was the chief abbot there at the monastery. I felt sure it would be good to follow her advice and I signed up for the Christmas two-week retreat of teachings. It was my first chance to stay at a Buddhist monastery with resident monks and nuns working to a formal timetable of daily prayers and activities.

Staying there and gaining an insight into monastic life and Buddhist teachings was exhilarating. The focal point was a large shrine room painted in bright colours and centred on a huge golden statue of the Buddha. While outside the winter weather of Scotland raged cold and dark, inside the shrine room were the colours of warmth and prayers of compassion. I was fascinated by the talks on Buddhist philosophy; it seemed so simple and sensible it was hard to see it as anything other than fact, to the point that I could see one might wonder if it was really a religion after all.

We suffer because we want things to be other than they are. If we start accepting, we free ourselves of this pattern of suffering. Don't harm and if you can always seek to help.

Still I wondered while it seemed easy to *know*, how easy was it to actually live?

I had heard that the actual man who became the Buddha did leave his worldly existence behind. He had had a wife and child and daily responsibilities and tasks. Leaving the retreat I was inspired but a little dubious as to how easy it was going to be to keep practising this philosophy back in the competitive world of finding a parking place in crowded Whitstable. Maybe it just was not really possible for someone like me, someone living a real life in the Western world…

Back in Whitstable, Peter and I had a hilarious time bumping a sanding machine into skirting boards as we attempted to revive the floor in my new home. We gave up and went out for supper.

Peter continued to work at his sculpture in a farm shed with a distinct lack of heating. I would pop in and marvel at how he could think straight in the midst of piles of wood dust and lumps of half-trees. He had also found his thing and was determined to carry it through, no matter how tough it got.

Alongside the office job, I returned to practising yoga on a weekly basis. After a few months I attended a local weekend yoga retreat while Peter was away installing a sculpture. At the end of the weekend two of my fellow students, Heather and Davina, approached me to ask if I would teach them. They explained that they had a local weekly yoga class but their teacher had moved away and they were keen to find a replacement. I was reluctant but they were so certain that I ended up agreeing. It was on a Monday night so I could easily do it after work.

I found that I now loved teaching yoga. Perhaps a few people spotted that and pretty soon others wanted to know if I could teach them too. So I decided, in mid-2002, to give up my office job and leap into being a self-employed yoga teacher. Peter and I designed a poster of a human figure in 'tree' pose (the one-legged standing posture with the other leg turned out with the heel on the inner thigh of the standing leg). Friends put the poster up and, from these small beginnings, a lot of classes quickly grew and eventually I was teaching fifteen classes a week. It felt a natural thing to do. I loved sharing something I believed in, something that I knew, from my own experience, could be of real help to people. Guiding students through breathing and postures and encouraging them to take time and feel present felt meaningful. Strangely it didn't seem to matter how things were with Peter, teaching yoga always brought out in me a voice of clarity. I was always able to teach because I was always speaking from the best part of me.

I decided to undertake further formal yoga-teacher training with the British Wheel of Yoga, a course of almost three years that covered many aspects of yoga and how to safely and sensitively teach physical yoga postures. It was exciting to glimpse how vast a subject yoga was, that it offered a lifetime of potential exploration. It was clear by the end of it that, as well as being flexible, I had a strong interest in meditation. They worked hand in hand – to sit to meditate you need to be physically comfortable and this is where my flexibility is really beneficial.

The course made me think about what 'yoga' was in general and for me in my life. From our study we learnt the word could mean many things, one of them the idea of being in a state of connection with your highest Self ('Self' with a capital S). Ultimately it was said that to be in this state could lead to a state of 'samadhi', the Sanskrit word for the final stage of yoga, associated with bliss and self-realisation. It also raised the fundamental question of what it is to be a yogi.

Reading the texts of yoga, its methods and possibilities seemed vast, far wider than I had imagined. For a yogi there are five possible methods or paths of yoga. They differ in nature but they all have in common the goal of self-realisation and freedom from the ego that I had started to read about. The five paths of yoga are: karma yoga, the yoga of selfless action; bhakti yoga, the yoga of devotion; raja yoga, the yoga of the mind or meditation; hatha yoga, the yoga of the body and the breath; jnana yoga, the yoga of study and knowledge.

Yogis in the West often become uncomfortable at the mention of yoga having a goal, as yoga is seen as a non-competitive, in-the-moment activity. It's true that these qualities are essential but it's also true that the classical texts of yoga state a clear goal: samadhi, a state of freedom from clinging to a little 'me'. Yoga's goal of self-realisation (samadhi) is broadly similar to the Buddhist notion of Enlightenment.

As most westerners starting yoga will tell you, the most accessible path tends to be that of hatha yoga. This path includes body and breath practices (asana and pranayama) as well as cleansing and concentration practices designed to take the practitioner towards samadhi. The broad path of hatha yoga is an umbrella term which includes ashtanga, iyengar, bikram and scaravelli yoga – all forms of hatha yoga because they all use the body and the breath as their chosen methods.

Beginning with the body is great because it's visible and it's easy to see what you're doing and why– something which tends to be rather trickier with the mind!

At first you concentrate on mastering your body's spatial movements... *Did they say left foot or right foot? Why is everyone else facing the door?* As you master the technicalities of where to place your body in space you can become aware of your breath. Then the breath and body can begin to work more closely together.

These practices are simple and wonderful. They are adaptable to a wide range of bodies and levels of fitness and, in emphasising the breathing, connect you to your natural relaxation system. As neuroscience tells us, the breath out (the exhale) is key in connecting a person to their parasympathetic nervous system, releasing chemicals which produce feelings of contentment. For people with busy lives which are increasingly driven by the fear-and-flight reactions of the sympathetic nervous system, yoga offers an enjoyable way to step out of anxious habitual reactions and the tight, restricted breathing patterns that go with them. Therefore in a very short amount of time, a new yogi can experience a different aspect of themselves, one which is more content and less exhausted by the habits of tension in the body and the breath.

In classical yoga writing the deeper, more internal practices tend to be done with a seated body, building up the mental muscles of concentration and meditation. There is a pathway in yoga, whichever path you take, that points to a mental state of being free of ego and, hopefully, a state of bliss.

The theory of the progression of yoga practices to this state is backed up by the yogic view of what it is to be a whole human being. According to yoga, every human consists of five sheaths, layers called 'koshas'. Imagine the koshas like the layers of an onion or a set of Russian dolls, one doll embedded within the other.

The most obvious aspect of a human being is the physical body; then there's the less visible but physically felt breathing kosha, similar to the Western notion of a person's nervous system; then the upper layers of a person's mind, centred on repetitive everyday thoughts. The next layer is interesting: the kosha of feelings and intuition, where there is less ego present and where the possibilities for deep kindness and wisdom exist. This fourth kosha and its development are the bridge which link to the final kosha, a state of limitless bliss where all selfishness has dissolved, connected to the Buddhist idea of your essential 'Buddha nature'.

Annamaya:
physical body

Pranamaya:
vital/breathing

Manomaya:
mental/thoughts

Vijnanamaya:
intuition/intelligence
moving towards wisdom

Anandamaya:
bliss/pure love and
realisation

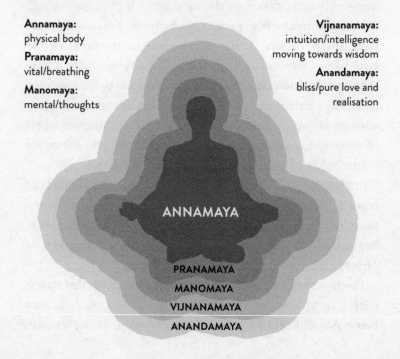

ANNAMAYA

PRANAMAYA

MANOMAYA

VIJNANAMAYA

ANANDAMAYA

CHAPTER 13

BLISS

Limitless bliss – I definitely wanted to know about that. Who doesn't? A bliss which does not go away but is a permanent state – and the texts said it was already there, an essential part of being a human.

It is hard not to wish for a fast track to this state, but there is no switch to flick that automatically lights it up like a Christmas tree shining at full throttle.

I recalled the Burmese reclining Buddha which had accompanied me on my long journey to this point. Is this what he had been showing me all those years ago? Had I been falling asleep under the shelter of a smile of bliss?

I mulled it all over as I got in the car to go shopping and noticed how tightly everyone seemed to be holding their steering wheels; how their unwatched faces looked so sad.

This yogic system of koshas was such a useful thing to stumble on. It offers a holistic way of explaining how to keep a human being totally well. It also explains why only talking on the residential course was not quite enough for me to recover completely from Jakarta. I needed yoga because it dealt with and helped all the layers of 'Emma'.

Inspired and keen to understand the three more mind-orientated koshas, I investigated Buddhism more seriously. Originating from North India and using so much of the yogic philosophy and methods, Tibetan Buddhism seemed inseparable from the teachings of yoga, placing particular emphasis on understanding the mind. It seemed to offer a way to understand yogic paths other than just the hatha yoga I had practised so far.

Buddhism also emphasises the importance of developing both kindness and a calm mind – the key elements in the fourth kosha. The development of kindness is not in any way exclusive to Buddhist thinking; it probably lies at the heart of all paths of faith or even non-faiths. We all know a kind person is a good person.

What Buddhism specifically seemed to offer, in a way that intrigued me, were books and prayers with guidance on the practicalities of how to develop true and stable kindness. I knew I needed clear guidance. I got the books but I was also aware that, in a perfect world, it would be great to find a teacher to help me make sense of it all. Where would I find a teacher to help me become a true yogi?

Under the smooth surface of my skin other parts of me wanted to grow. Perhaps a flower could bloom from a seed planted in the muddy darkness at the bottom of a lake a long time ago.

I formally became a Buddhist at the Kagyu Samye Ling Tibetan Monastery in Scotland on 1 January 2003. I took part in a ceremony in which Lama Yeshe cut a small piece of my hair and gave me a prayer string and a Buddhist name meaning Lamp of Bliss.

I walked outside on a cold Scottish afternoon and felt, if not an actual lamp, that a small flame had indeed begun to take light. It was something to do with kindness but I could not articulate exactly what.

I had taken time to make this decision because I had been clueless as to how the process of becoming a Buddhist worked. I'd also had a general reluctance to consciously join an institution of any type. Despite having been drawn to Buddhist teachings for a while, I wasn't sure what would be gained by *becoming* Buddhist. The question of how to officially become a Buddhist was fairly easy to answer; the question of what it meant to me to *be* a Buddhist, of how it would become a lived thing, was still unfolding.

When you are born in a non-Buddhist country, becoming a Buddhist requires taking part in a 'refuge ceremony'. The idea of taking refuge comes from the recognition that you are, despite the earth and sky, lost – in some sense a refugee looking for a home. I knew what it felt like not to be able to put your faith in buildings and watches and job descriptions – it was not so tough to accept the deeper need to place my faith elsewhere. I had had the tangible experience of crying for help, crying for my life, so I did not have an issue with asking for outside help. Perhaps I was a natural candidate for a religious point of view.

During the ceremony I took refuge in three things: the Buddha, Dharma and Sangha. The Buddha is the man who achieved enlightenment around the sixth century BC, the Dharma are the Buddhist teachings and the Sangha is the community of ordained and lay Buddhists. To become a Buddhist there needs to be a motivation to believe in these elements as support and inspiration in your internal development but the way in which that happens will be different for each person. Each individual will establish their connection to these three elements over time, helping them to understand and put into practice what it means for them to be a Buddhist.

The meaningful question for me about Buddhism was beginning to emerge although the wording was not quite clear: is it 'Be kind *and* calm your mind' or 'Be kind *to* calm your mind'?

I knew I was getting closer.

PART 3
SANGHA

CHAPTER 14

TRICKY, TRICKY

At points, usually when Peter and I were struggling, I did consider moving to the monastery or going travelling again. I vividly recall speaking, in the cafe at Samye Ling, to a woman who had been trekking in Bhutan. This country had always appealed to me. Tibet was naturally of interest to me but not to the extent that Bhutan was. If it had been easier to work out how to go I am sure I would have gone sooner but, as it was, it took a long time for this seed to grow fully.

I thought about becoming a Buddhist nun on one break from Peter, but only fleetingly and it was not obvious how to do so. The idea faded from my mind as Peter and I reunited and hope returned that a happy ending was still in sight. There was absolutely no one else I wanted to be with. There was no one like him. The best of me was the best of him.

It was just hard to make it work all the time. The relationship didn't seem to get any easier over time either because time had suspended within it little bits of angry debris. Nearly invisible bits of information floating in the air, ready to be plucked down and re-examined. The most infuriating thing was that my memory was still impacted from Jakarta so when Peter brought up something I had done wrong, I sometimes didn't remember it. We should have laughed and put on a couple of spotty bow ties but somehow we couldn't.

I discussed these emotional battles with my best friends. I was quite used to spending girl time discussing men; it's the default never-ending subject. Marilyn was a particularly patient friend of mine. A long-standing yoga teacher from Birmingham, she had a huge heart. She needed it as she must have thought she was on some kind of sponsored Groundhog Day. It was always a variation on the same theme.

By this stage a lot of my other friends were my yoga students and I didn't want to talk about my personal relationship with them. They were coming to me to relax, not get dumped on! So, although Marilyn was in Birmingham and we had to talk through a phone, it tended to be her I turned to.

I would sit on the bed at home or sit on the floor, back resting against the wall. Tired, wondering why things were so stuck.

Yet I would always end up repeating, 'I *do* love him, Marilyn.'

'Yes, honey, I know you do,' she would say with such warmth. 'What's happened now?' She would gently ask the reason for *this* call, today. And I would explain something about shopping not done or car keys lost or some small thing which had become so huge. I can't even remember now what seemed so colossal then.

'If I ask him to do something he just gets so huffy. Then I get defensive, then he gets huffy and there we go again; round and round...' I would sigh out, a sound trapped deep in my chest. '... No clue of how to really get out of it.'

Marilyn and I would talk calmly and helpfully in a way I wished Peter and I could. Always, feeling better, we would

say goodbye, both of us confirming, 'People in love are crazy.'
'Bonkers, more like.' Always wondering why love is so hard
when it's supposed to be the best thing, the thing to be aiming
for – right?

Marilyn described it like a wrestling position. 'It's being in
the grip of something, Em. You're in the grip of something.'

She was probably right.

Marilyn and I had met on a yoga breathing training course
and clicked immediately; one of those instant moments when
you feel at home with someone. We immediately relaxed
with each other and opened up like flowers on fast forward,
nodding over to talk to each other.

One of the wonderful things about a life turned towards
yoga was that I had begun to find friends at long last. People
I felt connected to. Marilyn was high up on that list. She was
part of a loose sangha, a community of like-minded people
I was beginning to find in my life. She lived in a rural area
near Birmingham with her husband and son, and was an
honest person with thick dark-blonde hair and a curvy shape.
Her general response to the difficulties of life included the
repetition, with untarnished wonder, of 'how weird life is'.

While these connections were building in the background
Peter and I became busy with our own stuff. We were busy in
the daytimes and also at weekends which meant there ended
up being little time for fun couple time, outside of sex. We
were dating and free of the pressure of the M word but still
it was tricky.

We decided to do some relationship counselling as the
pull-push tug of war was causing more conflict than peace.
It was telling that it was tough even trying to sort out our

diaries to find a time in the week when we could both attend counselling. Eventually sorted, counselling proved to be helpful but tricky because it encourages stagnating stuff to come up to the surface and rot in public. Three people hear it: the counsellor, your partner and you. I spoke and Peter spoke. It was useful to listen to each other, uninterrupted. It was a little scary too as I realised just how different we were and how differently we viewed things in the relationship. We talked a lot about the past. The past in our relationship usually felt heavy, like we were dragging some dying animal up on to the counsellor's sofa with us. It was the broken-off engagement.

What the counsellor said was good. I can see that now. She gave us little things to practise like showing and speaking words of appreciation to the other person, practising compromise. The reality was that when you love someone it can bring out the very worst in you. This was a real shock. I hated myself at times.

Who is this demanding, perfectionist, grumpy person?

How had being 'in love' caused this person to appear and squat in *my* body?

I wasn't surprised Peter was finding it hard to be with me. I was finding it hard to feel comfortable with the person I seemed to be.

I knew I wanted someone for me – just for me. I wanted this. I was no longer ambivalent, touch and go, happy with time apart/time together. I wanted someone that was Mine. I thought that this was the route to happiness, having that one person.

In fact, it seemed to make me possessive and horrid at points.

Yet *despite all this* we wanted to stay together – yes, there are probably books written on these strange dynamics (was it really just co-dependency?).

For me, confirming that in a positive way meant Making Plans For The Future. Although I had pre-empted the Big Questions of a relationship too soon, bringing them up at the time of the early, messy engagement, in the end there is just no getting away from the conversations about houses, locations and careers. A lot of it comes down to money. A lot of it comes down to what you expect life to look like. Both these factors tend to be influenced by the situation you grew up in and the wish to definitely repeat it or to definitely avoid it.

When we had these kinds of conversations differences were quick to appear. It was still hard for me to think that money did not bring safety. I wanted to live in a low-crime area and didn't mind paying for the idea of buying safety. Peter thought that meant spending too much money. We dug our heels in, pulling against each other in a tug of war, which ended in us both falling over, stuck in the mud. As a solution we stopped talking about those future things and concentrated on everyday life which was OK, but there was one Big Question which could not be avoided.

My biology and simple maths reminded me that I was going to be thirty-nine in mid-2005. As that year approached, the penny really dropped: I was running out of time to have a child, I didn't know if we could even have a child, and whether that happened wasn't under my or our control. My body was saying: *Have a baby. Have a baby now* like a pantomime audience screaming at me, warning that time was running out. Looking up tables about fertility and female age only served to confirm that my body was right to catch my attention.

For much of my previous adult life I had spent a lot of effort on *not* getting pregnant and so had probably ended up thinking that the minute I stopped using contraception I would easily conceive a child.

I was a little hesitant about childbirth itself – I still remembered those films of childbirth we were shown at school which involved a lot of screaming and people saying, 'push, push' as the rest happened off camera. But other women managed so of course it *had* to be possible for me.

But first the Getting Pregnant part. We 'tried' but nothing happened. The fact that nothing happened made me more anxious and as the weeks went on my concern only increased with the lack of easy success. A day or two late in the month, I would buy a pregnancy test, disappointed with the result and the consequent arrival of my period a day or two later.

Finally we went to the doctor and I was told to come in for blood tests. These told me that there was a problem. I didn't appear to ovulate regularly which would make becoming pregnant, particularly at my age, difficult without additional, medical help. I was offered an appointment with a fertility specialist and encouraged to research the details of a hormone stimulation treatment using a drug called Clomid.

This was difficult news for Peter and I to rest on our fragile foundations. We did not want to adopt. We wanted to make something that was 'ours' but it was not looking possible. I guess it forced a make-or-break moment and, after years of indecision, we finally called it quits. No marriage, no baby, no house, no point.

Letting go of the person I felt was likely to be the love of my life – the one I would reach out to in a poignant death scene on a hospital bed – was so hard.

I cried a lot.

I took a step back.

At this point I suppose I could have done many things but my self-esteem was in the toilet and I thought the best thing to do was to put my armour back on. I was not strong enough to turn this hurt into compassion and wisdom; to know how to go inside and come out stronger. So I looked outside and thought it best to put a suit back on. A rather tasteful, understated, blue business suit. It was another type of grieving.

CHAPTER 15

COMFORT FOOD

I rented my house out in Whitstable. It was too painful.

I stopped yoga teaching. It was too personal.

I talked to Human Resources back at my old job in the bank – some of the same people were still there. I was surprised to hear Morag say 'the door is never closed'. I talked to Bill (he of the watch). I met with Jim (he of the conversation in Hong Kong). I told them I missed using my brain, which I did. I explained that I missed the feeling of being part of something. What I did not mention is that I wanted to turn my back on everything that had gone before, to wash it out of me and down the drain with all the unwanted skin and hair circling downwards towards the sea.

I was lucky enough to be offered a job back in London with the bank, this time analysing other people's investment funds in the hedge fund sector. This part of the bank was situated off Piccadilly, close to Green Park, St James's Park and Buckingham Palace. It was a very nice part of town and different from the modern City of London further to the east.

I moved to a small flat in Pimlico within walking distance of the office. I bought a few expensive pieces at Max Mara on Bond Street in greys and blacks, and of course some new shoes. I became, again, a financial analyst. It was good in a well-if-you're-not-going-to-have-a-child-you-might-as-well-make-money way.

I needed to be a success in an obvious, outward way. This was my way of turning around the hurting. The failure of my relationship and the apparent loss of ever being a mother needed One Big Distraction if it was going to stop the hurting.

It was one of my turning points. East, west? Inwards, outwards?

I had spoken to Lama Yeshe at Samye Ling and seriously considered going into retreat to do the Buddhist practices of 'ngondro', the title for an intense set of Buddhist prayers and meditations undertaken by monks, nuns and serious lay students. But, in the end, returning to London seemed an easier path so I placed the thought of ngondro to one side. In retreat the mind needs to be stable and I am pretty sure my mind was not ready for extensive solitary meditation. Meditation is very tricky without a basic level of emotional stability in place.

In London, with a job which gave me clear tasks to undertake, I could leave my heart alone to recover of its own accord as I concentrated on achieving. It was a nice change to be employed and listening to instructions rather than self-employed and starting everything myself.

The pace of life in London did not allow much time for reflection, which was helpful. Once again the demands of focusing on financial facts and analysis gave me the simplicity of living in the analytically focused left-brain world. I had to work hard, learning a new area of finance and establishing a new role in a team. I put yoga and meditation practices on hold and took up running with the other female on the team, a French lady called Marie. It seemed a lot of people in the office ran and after a few days of sitting on my backside all day I could see why.

After a few weeks a woman on the settlements desk invited me out one evening. She said there was going to be a single bloke coming along and she thought it might be good for us to meet. I was happy to be invited. While getting to grips with the job I had mostly spent evenings on my own or at the gym – it's a City thing. I was not used to socialising after years of being with Peter or teaching yoga in the evenings so it was nice to feel that side of life might be picking up again.

We met after work one Friday night at a bar close to the office – there are some very nice bars around St James's Street. It was a small group of people: me, my colleague and three men. One of them was called Mark. He was tall with an appealing Scottish accent.

We all had drinks at the bar and then walked past the elegant stone buildings of St James's Street to go to a casino. I know it's giving my life an air of James Bond but this wasn't exactly known territory for me. In fact, I had only visited a casino once before, on the island of Macau off Hong Kong. HK had very strict rules on gambling so Macau functioned as a gambling sanctuary for those who had to go cold turkey in Hong Kong. In Macau the building had been functional outside with layer upon layer of gambling rooms inside. Each layer got more and more expensive to enter and had brighter and brighter patterned carpets reaching all the way up to the top of the building. I remember I sat next to a man who was so intent on the spinning of a wheel his eyes looked like glass. When he turned to look at me, in a pause, he had big gaps where some of his teeth were no longer in his mouth.

St James's Street on a warm evening in September 2005 was not like that at all. There were rich older East European men and young – I mean nineteen-year-old – women. The pattern was sighingly predictable.

Then there was us. We were chatting and drinking but not doing much gambling. Mark made an effort to get me a cappuccino – you see, I was never really a party girl. My silk shawl slipped as I put it round my shoulders as the evening drew to a close. He caught it and wrapped it round me, slightly squeezing the edges of my shoulders as he did so. My tummy did a back flip.

Interesting...

From that kindness things progressed. Mark was the polar opposite of Peter. He bought me elegant, white lilies and took me out to meals. I felt treasured in a way which was calm and reassuring. More like the kind of relationship my own mother and father had had where there was enough money to do things you wanted and there was a sense of teamwork. I liked the feeling of romance. I liked that he remembered to shave and drove a car not filled with old receipts and wood chippings.

We had a lot in common; we had both spent time in Hong Kong and knew Asia well. We both worked in banking. There was clear ground to walk on together.

At that time he was in the process of divorcing his wife, a change which had obviously left him hurting and his self-esteem bruised. So we also had this in common. Our insides probably mirrored each other's and perhaps we recognised that – recognised it in each other. Maybe because of this feeling of familiarity, we both acted quickly, jumping into a relationship.

Come on let's start running....

As usual I was the one who was keen to get something definite sorted out and I did like Mark, but even so I struggled with the relationship from quite early on.

Keep trying...

I had probably not had anywhere near enough time to recover from Peter. Peter and I had been interconnected for a long time and had been through a huge range of experiences and emotions. It was foolish to think I would be ready in a few weeks to start again as if magically healed with London glue and new clothes.

How do I stop this?

Perhaps it is easy to see it now, but it was hard to fully see at the time. And the horrid thing is that when you enter a relationship soon after a previous one, you spend a lot of mental time making comparisons. Comparing the present to the past; what you have with what you had. As Einstein pointed out, there's no getting away from relativity. I imagined that the opposite type from last time *must* be the right type. This approach to human relationships was silly and two-dimensional. It was not going to work.

I am not sure if it is possible to ever cleanly and easily end a relationship. It's not like closing a door on an untidy bedroom or pressing a waste-disposal button. *Slam, clunk,* done.

Things stay with you and drift out to recapture your attention. The power of old habits: to still want to call his number, still want to share things with *him* first. Added to which the tendency, as time passes, to remember the good bits and drop the bad bits. With a memory like mine I caught myself not even being sure why we had split up in the first place.

I called Marilyn a fair bit.

We were to spend Christmas 2005 with Mark's parents up in Scotland. We had committed to this plan right at the woozy beginning, weeks earlier. As the time approached I began to feel anxious about it. I knew the relationship was causing me tension or that my tension was causing the relationship... Anyway, whatever the precise cause-effect thing that was going on, I wish I hadn't said I would go. His parents were lovely and kind, and I was so sorry but I just wanted to be on my own. I felt trapped at the Christmas table. I felt rubbish that their hopes for me were not ones I would be able to fulfil.

I *know* I am impossible. Perhaps I was beginning to finally realise that no matter how much I wanted love I didn't seem to be able to commit – yes, I know there are books on this too! I wondered if wanting a meaningful life and wanting a partner were not the same thing at all. Well, not for me anyway.

I had to have the courage to make my own decision. Just after New Year 2006 I told Mark it was over. It had been a short relationship, only a few weeks, but intense with my undercurrent of wanting and worrying. I knew it was not right for me. I had done enough puzzles to know a piece can look right but sometimes, even when you squeeze it and want it to fit perfectly, it just isn't. You have to put it back on the pile and take another look at the picture on the box.

CHAPTER 16

A NEW LIFE

It seems though that the sun is always there, warming the ground, even when the clouds are out. Everything had been put in place and, even at that point, I was being pulled towards the greatest of loves and the deepest of meanings. A few days after speaking to Mark, I discovered I was going to become a mother.

Given my previous medical prognosis combined with my newly single state, I was stunned. I did three pregnancy tests, buying them on my lunch break, hoping no colleagues were at *this* Boots, just over the road from the office. I paused as I digested the small blue lines on the pregnancy tests, looking at them lying in a row on the floor of the loo cubicle at work.

I called my doctor, who was equally surprised.

I decided to call Mark to tell him. Although we had split it was the right thing to do.

'Mark, can you talk?'

'Yup. What's up?'

'Mark, I'm pregnant.' It was such a small sentence to speak down the phone in the midst of a workday.

'What? Are you sure?'

'Yes,' I said, leaning on the built-in sink unit with my back turned away from the taps. I had the place to myself.

'That's amazing.'

'I know.'

We arranged to meet the next day.

I went back to sit at my desk aware of this huge secret I was now holding in me. I was so excited but I also felt a sense of dread. I knew that I did not want to be with Mark and, sadly, having a baby did not change that.

The next day, trying to do all those centring things like walking slowly and checking my breathing, I set off on my lunch break to walk down Piccadilly. A ten-minute walk away I chose a metal stool at the back in the popular grab-and-go Pret a Manger. I was there first and I could see my reflection in the shiny metal counter as I sat waiting for him.

After a few moments, surrounded by busy people grabbing sandwiches I saw him arrive. He was wearing an expensive, fawn raincoat of the kind traditional City men like to wear. I had still hoped that, when he walked through that door, it would all be OK. That I would be able to jump up and declare, 'Yes, I want to start a family life with you, Mark. Yes, with *you*.' But I didn't feel that way and I stayed on my metal stool and had to gently explain this despite the excitement we shared at the news.

Mark was gutted that I did not want to restart the relationship despite this change in circumstance. I am sure that was tough for him.

It was a shock for my family to hear that I had both ended the relationship and become pregnant so close together. My mum couldn't quite understand why I couldn't go back 'for the sake of the child'. But I knew I couldn't and that if I did, the baby would without doubt go through a horrid parental split when it was growing up. Better to have it like this.

At thirty-nine I was classed as an 'older mother'. It was nice to know I was already a mother even though I had yet to endure any physical pain! At any age pregnancy brings confusion and excitement and mine was no exception. My body, which I had become fairly familiar with, took on a life of its own (no pun intended) and started popping out in all kinds of new places. I had nausea from six weeks right up until I completed giving birth. They call it morning sickness but mine wasn't well mannered enough to leave by lunchtime.

It was a strange thing, being pregnant on my own. I experienced the oddness of not having someone immediately close by to discuss plans and exciting details with, or to share worries and decisions with. I admire anyone who is a parent and certainly anyone who raises a child largely on their own. It's an understatement to say it's a big job. It's so big I can't find the words. I am still amazed the human race has kept going as long as it has. Mark and I managed to talk and prepare for the future. He wanted to take on the responsibilities that were soon to arrive and I was really pleased he wanted to play a big part in the baby's life.

I continued the daily walk to work from my flat in Pimlico, starting each day over breakfast looking at the picture book which showed what was happening on that particular day of a baby's growth. The 'morning sickness' continued to be hideous and sitting upright to slumped at a computer did not feel a great thing to be doing with the bouts of acid air that were coming up. But yet I still loved the job; we were going out interviewing investment professionals and writing up our recommendations on who to invest with. I felt a little self-conscious as I began to bring a larger and larger tummy with me to such a non-Mothercare setting but I was probably far more aware of it than anyone else.

I celebrated my fortieth birthday on 16 July 2006, gathering Mum, Lucy and her family, my brother, Toby, and friends at a local restaurant back in Whitstable for a big lunch. Marilyn, her husband, Ron, and son, Alex, even came down from Birmingham for it – staying the weekend in a beachside B&B. It was a great day of bringing lots of people together and celebrating with my ever-larger bump fitting under the lunch table.

The next day I was due to go for a routine check-up at the hospital where I was scheduled to give birth a couple of months later.

Marilyn told me later that Mum had expressed concerns about my pregnancy to her over the birthday lunch. She had confided in her that she was worried it was not all going OK. Once again Mum was right!

Just before leaving for the check-up I started bleeding and it wasn't from my nose. On arrival at hospital I was quickly seen and it was discovered the baby 'was in distress', which is a horrible phrase and a precursor to all the years of guilt I was about to feel as a mum for not doing a good enough job.

I was hospitalised. It was discovered that the baby was not growing correctly and was severely undersized for its age. I had injections and was told to prepare for a child with medical issues and/or an elective C-section to get the baby out soon if things did not improve. They thought the blood flows to the baby were not working quite right.

I was told to immediately stop work. I phoned the office and told them I could not come back. That was that.

I phoned the landlady of the Pimlico flat and arranged to stop my lease early.

I was scared stiff.

How on earth will I cope? A baby with potential special needs and doing it all on my own?

I didn't feel up to the challenge, even though it was only a theoretical worry brought on by discussions with the doctors.

What is going to happen?

I so wanted to be a mum but had just not imagined this might be the way it would go.

After a stay in hospital I was allowed to leave as long as I went on bed rest. The only exception to this would be to travel back and forth to the hospital every day for scans to see if it was still safe for me to continue carrying the baby.

I moved in with Mum, who was still living in our family home in Whitstable. Heavily pregnant, I went back to the house we had all grown up in. At the other end of Whitstable, various things were being delivered to my own house. I had followed up on the medical advice to buy a bed (I had still only got a mattress on the floor) and an actual table and chairs (I had been eating at a low table off cushions) as the surgery of a caesarean would make these low-lying habits too tricky.

It was late summer but back at Mum's I mainly stayed indoors doing puzzles with a fan close by to keep me cool. It was not easy to be left alone with my thoughts. After what the hospital had said, I was terrified that I was going to be on my own dealing with a child with serious medical issues. I was not sure I was strong enough to cope with that. But no one knew. No one could give me a definite idea of what to expect; it was just possibilities which had been raised.

Mum bought a mobile phone, which was a big deal for someone in their seventies who thought these objects were 'ghastly'. Trying to familiarise herself with it she made a big muscular effort when learning how to press the numbers on it, holding them individually for a long time as she sounded out the relevant number. It was best not to sigh.

Luckily an emergency call was not necessary. I rested and scanned and rested and scanned and managed to keep carrying the baby until thirty-nine weeks.

By the time I went into labour, all I could focus on was getting through it; physical pain certainly overrides fear! I so wanted to hold the baby I had been carrying through finance meetings and London streets and then which had waited as I sat, under doctor's orders, through endless puzzles and super-slow walks in hospital car parks.

When I had been hospitalised back in July I had had the strongest feeling that this child should be called Oscar. Previously when Mark and I had talked about names, Daniel had seemed a good choice. But now, faced with an imminent emergency delivery, I phoned Mark and said I thought we should call him Oscar. So that's who we were waiting for. Oscar is a Nordic name meaning 'Spear of God'.

On the evening of 14 September 2006, the waiting was finally over and Oscar decided it was his time to arrive. After all the blood and screaming and breathing and pushing, he was in my arms. I was cradling a new world in which tears meant joy and small meant enormous. I was terrified he was going to lack a limb or show some of the problems the doctors had said might well arise but he was perfect. He was small at five pounds four ounces – but perfect. I could not believe it.

So hugely relieved and thrilled, I called Mark to tell him that he had a son; Oscar had made his entrance. It was a drawn-out entrance, having said that – it took him thirty hours to arrive, far longer than it took Mark to get to the hospital in Maidstone.

Sitting in the hospital bed the next day in a pair of pink, collarless Mothercare pyjamas, I waited for Mark. The bed was narrow with light grey, rounded metal bars to stop you falling out. Beside me in a transparent cot lay Oscar, fragile but well wrapped-up with the swaddling technique the nurses said made babies feel secure.

I was nervous to see Mark. My hormones and emotions were jumping about under the stains on my pyjamas. I had not seen him for a good two or three months.

It was easy to spot Mark arriving, his tall frame smart in a dark blue blazer. He seemed huge from the perspective of a propped-up-in-bed person. He impressed the other mums on the ward as he walked by – clearly they thought I had 'a catch' there. He stood looking over at Oscar sleeping in his little see-through plastic cot. I don't think either of us believed we had really done it. We really had made this new little person. We were both filled with wonder at a world which now had our son in it.

He must have thought I held all the cards, lying there next to the baby which had been growing inside me. But inside I did want protection, a solid arm, someone to help me with this and here he was in front of me – *here* was Oscar's father.

I nearly reached out to Mark as he stood there so proud and lost. It was hard. I so nearly did. But in the end, no. I knew it would be impossible. It would lead to unhappiness for all of us. I said nothing more and, after our goodbyes, I watched him walk away, past the other mums and babies. I could not rely on my history or the married example of my own mum and dad. This was not going to be the way. Mark and I would have to make it work together – apart.

I had to get some grit and determination from somewhere even if it meant remembering those cowboy films Dad liked to watch. The ones with the solitary guy, his legs set like concrete posts, standing on the main street of a dusty town, ready to do whatever it took. I wasn't sure I needed Dad quite like that though; maybe I just needed him comfortably settled on our sofa in Whitstable. But I wished he were there. I wanted his help and I also wanted to show him Oscar, his grandchild.

Come on Emma you can do this.

Mum drove us home from hospital very slowly at my insistence. Every other person seems hell-bent on careering into you with their over-fast tank-vehicle when you first get in a car with your newborn in a little carrier.

Oscar and I went to my house in Whitstable to make it *our* house. At last I had done something right.

Once home my little boy slept by me in a small basket before moving into an official cot in his own room. Despite having looked at all those pictures in the baby books, I wasn't well prepared for the actual tasks of looking after this small human being; maybe no new mother is. I was worried I might break his little skinny limbs as I washed him in a

special hand bath the size of a watering can. A convulsive fit
brought on by a high temperature late at night when he was
eight weeks old was terrifying and required the ambulance.
Teething was incessant and *so much* for not having a baby that
cried – clearly he was learning to use his lungs. I absolutely
adored him *and* it was tiring. What had I thought was so
tough about spreadsheets and marketing meetings? Two-
hour meetings and deadlines seemed like a luxury break now;
I could eat them for breakfast now – except I was knackered,
and breakfast with Oscar took about two hours!

For the first year after Oscar's birth I was on maternity
leave from my job. The after-work drinks in central London
and the urgent processing of reports were far away from my
car-seat-pram-sling modes of existence. I pushed him around
Whitstable and along the beach. I made new friends, mums
with babies born at the same time. Together we swapped
tips and helped each other get through the tiredness and
the teething.

I loved carrying Oscar in his sling attached to my front,
his gorgeous, dimpled toes and fingers peeping out from it.
I understood why people said babies were so beautiful you
could eat them. The force of love was incredible. It was the
time of a huge heart pumping away, comforting Oscar, and a
brain which felt as if it had shrunk in the tumble dryer.

After that first year I went back to work in London,
commuting from Whitstable. It was no problem fitting
back into my old suits; the first months of caring for Oscar
had been like boot camp workouts. My face looked more
knackered though; it would have taken surgery to get rid of

the eye bags which had become an extra feature on my face. On my worst days I must have had a bit of a bloodhound look going on above the neck.

I definitely wanted to go back to work, to have a job of that kind. I wanted to use my analytical brain again and spend some time among adults. Plus, I needed to work to help support us financially and the pay in London was far greater than locally. I hired a very experienced local nanny, Julia, to take care of Oscar on the three days I left Whitstable on the train, bound for the London office.

Commuting from Whitstable to a job in central London, even though it was only part-time, was the closest I've ever come to being a plate-juggling clown. I am sure that many people working in an office environment with a young baby at home feel they are part of a slapstick comedy routine, their bodies half suited and half vomited on.

Lots of people had said the same thing: 'You get used to the commute.' It was one hour and twenty minutes between Whitstable and London. In total that amounted to two hours and forty minutes sitting on a train, added to which there were the walks at either end of the journey. I started the habit of commuting feeling positive, determined to use the time constructively to read or work. I ended up flicking through the pictures of a free newspaper grabbed at the station, my internal organs slumping like a tired child on a long car journey.

I would get up at six in the morning to have breakfast and get ready. The nanny would come at 6.30 and I would walk to the station in trainers with my heels in a bag. Once at Victoria Station I would quickly walk to the office and arrive there, one of the last people to arrive as most of the teams lived closer by in London. By the time I sat down at my desk to look at private equity fund documents I felt as if I had achieved a lot and fancied lunch.

Then, due to the need to get back to take over from the nanny, I had to leave the office by 4.30 p.m. I felt as if I should either whistle like one of the Seven Dwarfs or shrink like a decompressed milk container as I walked out past the desks with single people still working away at them. I used to be one of those people but I wasn't now. Now I had a child who needed me. I felt embarrassed that I could not stay until 7 or 8 or go for after-work drinks any more. It wasn't that I didn't want to but I just could not. I felt like I was skiving when in fact I was actually being a plate-juggling superhero.

Working part-time was great but also had an unsatisfactory edge as there was the inevitable important meeting you missed or something you weren't brought up to speed on. It seemed rather unprofessional to have to keep asking what your own team was up to. Perhaps if I had not known anything else, had not known what it felt like to make the decisions, to be *essential*, I would not have minded, but I did. It was a diluted version of work or life or both which was also overwhelming at the same time.

I enjoyed being back at work, acquiring facts and theories through the analysis of funds and companies. I still liked asking questions, investigating people to understand what they were doing and why they were doing it. If I could have just separated my head from my body and my life it would have been fine but of course this was not an option. Everything was connected.

Recognising the connections didn't make it any easier though, so, after a year of baby in one hand and spreadsheet in the other, it felt too tough. I felt too old for it and realised I had created a life which was not sustainable over the long term. I decided to base myself full time in Whitstable with Oscar, with the support of my mum and sister, Lucy, close by. I got on with the day-to-day stuff of life – and caught up on sleep.

After a few months I made the decision to return to self-employment and teaching yoga. I was nervous that I had forgotten how to teach after nearly three years away from it, but it was good. Coming back to it was easy. It also gave my life flexibility in terms of looking after Oscar. It didn't feel a less adequate version of something better. It felt right.

With Oscar beginning to spend pockets of time at pre-school I was able to teach a little yoga in the daytime. I taught differently, perhaps more compassionately, now with the eyes of a parent. Many of the students coming to class were juggling so many roles and finding that tough, particularly in terms of being parents. They needed time to relax and refresh in order to carry on.

Gradually yoga and an interest in Buddhism seeped back into my life, once the bulk of daily laundry (vomit, bed wetting, carrot puree) decreased. In reading more of the yogic and Buddhist philosophy I had to reflect on the nature of a spiritual path and the question of what gives a human life meaning. I had put these elements to one side in my brief return to work in London and in the morning-sickness months before Oscar, now I was ready to bring them back in.

In reflecting on things and talking to students I became increasingly aware that parenthood could be seen in opposition to the spiritual. Now I run into people who say, with a clear sense of apology, they have given up meditating because of looking after children. But it was already becoming so clear to me that the path of a parent requires the greatest commitment of love and patience. In this way it seemed to offer the chance to free yourself of the self-centred trap which the Buddhist texts kept reminding me to get out of.

The act of giving birth itself seemed to have begun this process. Having stretched and pushed and screamed to get that new life felt like the shedding of an old self. As a parent you now take second place in your own mind. The child comes first. It has to. It can do nothing without you, except pooh and throw up. You run around putting the child down, picking it up, making the food, feeding the food, clearing up the food, wiping the bottom, changing the nappy, making up bottles, washing up bottles. And kissing it and holding it and loving it. All while you wait for it to grow up and be able to drive its own car and cook its own pizza and read its own books.

As time has gone on I've become more and more aware of how bonkers it seems to separate parenthood from a spiritual path and I continue to see the role of a parent as rich in potential for the deepest of understandings. It's not one of the five forms of yoga but maybe it should be.

CHAPTER 17

THE IMPORTANCE OF KINDNESS

The very first principle of yoga is 'ahimsa'. This Sanskrit word, made famous by Gandhi, means non-violence, compassion or, simply, kindness. This word has a long history in the texts of yoga, particularly in Patanjali's yoga sutras, that text Dave had begun to whisper to me by the sea in Australia years back.

Remember ahimsa. Before any action, posture, meditation, before *anything*. For me this continues to be the most powerful guidance when dealing with any everyday situation. I try to make it and remake it as my starting place.

It's easy to say it as you slowly breathe out. *Ah-him-sa*. It lessens the likelihood of me hurting others and then experiencing the pain of regret. It saves me from clearing up a whole lot of mess I would otherwise easily make. In the Buddhist texts this link was clearly explained. Practising kindness was seen as something which calms the mind in and of itself, and not practising it leaves the mind jumpy and ill at ease. I had not appreciated that practising kindness was not just a moral thing but of deep benefit to the practitioner in the way it keeps the mind calm and undisturbed. In this way it seemed clearly linked to meditation. This was interesting as

I had probably assumed that the only way to calm the mind was to sit quietly and meditate.

It wasn't easy to remember in the first three years of bringing up Oscar though. There were many moments when ahimsa felt like an impossible path. I was saved by the rope of love tied round my middle, dragging me up and over the challenge of unforeseen circumstances that I felt woefully unprepared for. The yoga path of love was profound but it didn't stop me from crying or feeling pissed off when the pram wheel ran over dog pooh and a lack of sleep made opening drawers with child-proof locks impossible. Oscar was beginning to show himself more clearly as the months progressed. He was frequently described by strangers as 'a handful', 'a live wire', as they held their bags a little closer as if he might whip them off their elbow and bash them round the head. He would need to constantly tap things, fiddle with things.

I didn't think too much of it. He *was* a boy and I could see that bringing up any child was jolly hard work. I suppose differences became more obvious with nursery school, where it's easy to compare your own child to the others in the line. After a few months of pre-school it became clear the teachers were finding him hard to manage and, when he turned four, a special educational advisor was brought in to begin to assess him. He seemed to have difficulties in managing himself physically. I knew autism existed but only vaguely and was grateful for the involvement of Jan, the educational advisor at the school, and I watched to see how things developed.

Placing these moments of anxiety aside, my interest in meditation and yoga were deepening. This was partially because managing Oscar was proving quite hard work and words like 'patience' and 'empathy' were taking on a whole new dimension called *reality*. Ahimsa was hanging on by a thread.

Oscar's nanny, Julia, who continued to help out before he joined school, also mentioned she thought he was rather unusual. I had not had a child before, or even extensive experience with children, so when she began to express some concerns I listened. I knew she wasn't blinded by love in the way that I was. In the last stages of the pregnancy when the doctors thought Oscar might be born with a serious physical issue, I had been terrified. When he arrived with all ten toes and fingers and nothing unusual about his physical movements, I had, with an enormous sigh of relief, happily assigned these concerns to history. It did not occur to me that some other problem might show up later on.

After a series of assessments Oscar was given a diagnosis of attention deficit hyperactivity disorder. Sounds like a load of old codswallop to some – apparently, from newspaper articles I've glimpsed – but, sadly, it isn't. ADHD. Another set of four letters ending with 'disorder'.

I remembered the doctors after the PTSD residential asking if I was planning to have children and cautioning me that it may be difficult due to my experiences. I didn't go into this point in depth with them at the time. My pregnancy had been fairly stressful; this might have contributed, the doctors thought, to the arising of Oscar's condition. Or maybe my Buddha wanted me to work out a path to happiness and knew that without obstacles I would never understand anything.

I looked for a *why* for a bit, but not for too long. I was too busy doing my best to bring him up. Learning to help

Oscar and gaining the strength needed to manage him have undoubtedly been reasons why I needed to deepen my spiritual understanding. I have cried, hit walls, shouted, left play dates, thought of walking away, apologised time and time again. These were my original reactions and methods but they have changed. We have both grown up. At this stage he had the diagnosis but medication was not an option. It was only later, at the age of six, he was prescribed medicine and that has helped hugely. I am so grateful to the scientists who invented that. It gives him a decent stab at sitting down long enough to cope with being at school.

Some days it seems like Oscar is just an extreme version of us all as we play endlessly with iPhones, twitching every few seconds at their sounds and vibrations. Other days I watch his difficulty with sitting, his need to hit something constantly, his struggle to control his own self. It's painful to watch.

A part of me, at first, felt embarrassed at his behaviour and at the fact that he had this condition. It was not the type of child I wanted to have. Hey, I was a cool yogi; why was this whirling dervish making me look like a rubbish parent?

Oscar's behaviour makes it appear as if he has been brought up with no effort and no rules. This has not been the case but mentioning ADHD has often brought judgement in reply. Parenthood offers such potential for expansion of heart and mind, but it's very easy for these good qualities to centre only on one's child, even to the detriment of others. It's a trap I am all too aware of as a parent and a Buddhist practitioner.

Understanding of ADHD (still often known as ADD, Attention Deficit Disorder) is developing, just as it is for dyslexia and Asperger's and a range of issues which arise from the many potential structures of a human's brain. While the cause of ADHD is not currently clear, there is increasing evidence from neuroscientists that children with ADHD have different brain wiring. There is significant research being carried out on the links between PTSD and ADHD. I don't want to make an easy cause-effect conclusion but there are strands which link them together and I wonder if yoga and meditation are also very effective in the managing of both.

It's thought that, in ADHD, the frontal cortex of the brain develops more slowly, delaying the development of key control functions such as planning, memory and attention. It's also thought that the neurotransmitters in these brains work differently; it's a cutting-edge area of research. It helps to know of this research but on a day-to-day level I still have to understand and manage Oscar. My job is to encourage him and help him understand the impact of his behaviour on himself and others. I love him hugely and I know he will be OK in the end. He will grow up and the high waves will become calmer and he will find the pieces to his jigsaw.

If I sound defensive it is because I am a lioness protecting my cub. I want my child to be free of difficulty. I want to take *all* possibility of suffering away.

I have already seen how hard it has been for Oscar socially, at school in lessons, and have heard others' responses towards him. It's hard for people to deal with Oscar – including me! – because they don't want a fidgety, noisy child around them, and they find it hard to stay peaceful and happy when surrounded by fidgety behaviour. People are unsettled by *his* unsettledness – it seems to be contagious and, as always when our minds are unsettled by outer circumstances, it's harder to practise kindness. In such situations I have to find a way through, a way which remembers that all parenting is hard. If it wasn't, we might be more content and less vulnerable to passing on our own frustrations.

As Oscar sung to me, 'Twinkle, twinkle, little star, what you say is what you are'.

He had a lot worked out at an early age.

Motherhood has been a big shovel that dumped me 100 per cent on to a spiritual path. That's OK. Don't they say the person you love should bring out the best in you?

Digging deep for Oscar and turning to my amassed library of Buddhist books for strength and guidance, I thought more of places of peace, places of calm and simple quietness. I thought again about the Himalayan country of Bhutan. Perhaps this was why it appealed. A canvas I could project my wish for peace on to.

I still had limited knowledge of what Bhutan was like but the word 'Bhutan' appealed to me; it struck my ears and made them perk up like a satellite dish looking for a signal. Bhutan, Bhutan... what *is* that word registering in my head?

It was ridiculous that I had not yet gone there given the number of times the thought of it had risen to the surface over the years. The combination of the expense, not having anyone to go with and not knowing how to actually do it had acted as obstacles. Added to which, as you have seen, there had been a fair amount of life activity. All in all, it meant I still hadn't gone to Bhutan *yet*.

In our late teens, sitting in my yellow attic room, my sister, Lucy, and I had written a list of our life dreams. By 2011 we had both achieved a lot of them. Lucy has yet to have a herb garden and I think I'd better let go of the idea of my own swimming pool but, through work and my extensive yoga travels, I had seen many countries (high on my list), but Bhutan was still missing.

I had run into a few people who had been to the country but I had not had a chance to learn about it in depth. No one I knew in Whitstable had been. It was hard to demystify Bhutan. I got some books and began to read about it properly.

Bhutan had an uninterrupted history as a Buddhist country. The photos were of a mountainous country with colourful prayer flags strung through skies and extraordinary cliff-top monasteries with golden roofs. Brochures showed the red robes of monks and nuns set against lush green paddy fields and smiling. Always there was the smiling. So this was Bhutan; looking back at me.

Oscar and I went on a package holiday in Spain. There was a great kids' club for him and it meant a break from household chores for me. I enjoyed getting hot on a sun-lounger while reading about Bhutanese takins, their national animal. I smelt of sun lotion and Oscar loved the 'international' buffet with shiny prawns so big they looked like they might turn into earrings.

The book on the sun lounger described a place of kindness and simplicity where parts of the country still lived what looked like a medieval, subsistence lifestyle, close to nature. There were facts about the government's legislated requirement to keep a large part of the country forested so it remained a place of riches for plants, animals, birds and butterflies. There were frequent festivals with sacred dances, costumes and huge paintings rolled down the front of buildings. It was an entirely Buddhist country of 700,000 people which had remained largely closed to the outside world until the 1970s. A world unlike any I had encountered.

I decided it was time. I had to go.

The idea of such long-distance solo travel had seemed impossible when Oscar was small, when even getting to the shops had felt like an assault on the steep side of the Eiger. With Oscar now turning five, it began to seem possible though.

I looked into tours offered by specialist travel companies – this was definitely a different market from all-inclusive Canaries holidays in the sun. I found a company taking groups to Bhutan led by Zara Fleming, a specialist in Buddhist art. I decided this was the trip for me.

Luckily two of my yoga students, Karin and Bridget, decided to join me. Karin was also a Buddhist practitioner and Bridget was leaning that way so we were all interested in exploring a fully Buddhist culture. We signed up for the October 2011 itinerary. Going in this way, with a group and a guide, seemed the only route in.

Oscar was attending school by this point and, between my mum and Mark, he would be well taken care of while I was gone. In the run-up to departure I had a few wobbles, wondering if it was wise to go, if I was being a rubbish mother. I even thought about cancelling, but Mum told me in no uncertain terms, 'Now, Emma, I am quite bored enough with hearing how much you want to go to Bhutan. Please just go! Everything will be fine.'

Mums sometimes do know best.

CHAPTER 18

NEW PEAKS AND TROUGHS

I packed an enormous amount of different clothing suitable for every range of temperature into a new suitcase and Karin and I got a lift up to the airport in her husband's big truck. Sitting high up above the other vehicles on the M25 added to the feeling that we were off to jump into the unknown. At Heathrow we joined the rest of our group at the start of our organised schedule. It was to be a two-week journey, taking in Kathmandu in Nepal, Sikkim, parts of Northern India and ending with a few days in Bhutan.

We travelled first to Delhi and slumped wearily on a big round plastic sofa in the airport watching, dazed, as other travellers walked past duty-free and coffee outlets. Then we flew on to Kathmandu, the capital of Nepal.

Once through Nepalese immigration we arrived in the city of Kathmandu late at night and, in darkness, we travelled to a hotel called The Yak and Yeti. A man played the piano beautifully in the bar after supper. Outside there were lots of stalls selling T-shirts and flip-flops.

The next morning we went on a tour of the capital. We left the hotel in a coach and were taken into the middle of the city.

Karin and I had been chatting away, not taking a lot of notice of where we were, consulting a guidebook on what to see in Kathmandu. Suddenly the coach stopped and we grabbed our bags, heads full of pictures of ancient Nepalese statues strewn with garlands of orange flowers.

But what we saw as we got out were children. We were immediately surrounded by maimed children, their half-legs bouncing on wooden crutches. Some were propelling their half-bodies along on basic skateboard-type structures, using their fists to push themselves along the concrete. Children with legs that stopped at the knees, intent on keeping pace with us as we left the coach, scuttling along, incapacitated and desperate at our feet. The sight of this, particularly knowing my own child was safely back in England, was unbearably sad. I was totally lost for words.

We were told that many of these children had been deliberately maimed by their own families in order to increase their begging prospects. I do not know if these tales are true or not, but, whatever the causes behind what we were seeing, it was ghastly; a realm of hell in anyone's book.

It stopped me in my tracks; there I had been, nicely doing the compassion practice at home at the same time as these children stumbling painfully through life every single day. I had to wonder what mattered most. Was action more important than hopes or words? It brought the question of the nature of kindness right into the centre of the picture; not as a nice-to-have extra but as something which could make the difference between life and death, suffering and freedom.

Despite the fascination of Kathmandu and Sikkim the impact of these first few moments of the trip remained with me as we travelled on into Bhutan. Perhaps if I had stayed longer and seen these children again and again I would have been able to normalise it. I don't know. As it was, the memory of their staggered movements stayed with me, close to me. Again I was witnessing a suffering I felt fairly helpless to do anything about, let alone remove. It touched a place of sorrow in me and also dug a little into a dormant wish to help.

Being part of a group journey was a new experience for me. Before I had travelled alone, with Peter or perhaps a family member. Encountering strange places with strange people was all part of the mystery. I am sure all of us came on the trip for our own reasons, interested in particular areas. I was definitely the 'want to talk to a monk about meditation' traveller. Luckily I had Karin to share this aim with.

Both Karin and I were doing a short daily practice of compassion training. This training uses a visualisation, a prayer and the mantra *Om mani peme hung*. (You can see the mantra also written as *Om mani padme hum* but often the pronunciation is closer to *Om mani peme hung*; a mixture of Sanskrit origins with Tibetan intonation. However the precise spelling, this mantra is designed to focus the practitioner's intention on developing compassion. A practice which is thought to at one time develop the wish to help others and benefit the development of happiness and joy in one's own mind.)

Due to the ease of forgetting to practise kindness, the emphasis is on *deliberately* practising kindness, until it truly becomes our natural response. In doing this, the mind turns towards positive thinking and away from negative patterns of thought. This can then help free the individual from their own pains caused by thinking-of-self and create a more deeply meaningful life. It is the deliberate training in compassion through various methods and prayers just as you would train and deepen your understanding of any skill. While all humans are believed to have the full potential for unlimited kindness and wisdom, only through application and understanding will this part of themselves be freed to shine through.

The emphasis on compassion also brings the mind of the practitioner back to consider the motivation for their own life, which is to help other beings – not because you want to be a goody two shoes – but because true joy lies in being of service to others. This approach is not exclusive to Buddhism, nor indeed exclusively religious, but speaks profoundly to the potential of all human hearts.

So compassion practices are a very popular one throughout the Himalayas, among both monastic and lay people. You see endless people holding mala beads (or rosaries, as some might call them) and turning these beads with their left hand as they say the sounds *Om mani peme hung*. They may not know all the visualisations or be able to read texts on these compassion practices but they know this is the practice to help all beings and they do it. They don't do it secretly either, while no one else is watching. They do it anywhere, sitting on chairs outside shops, walking around chortens and monastic buildings, sitting in airport lounges and fields. They do it because they know everyone around them knows exactly what they are doing and because they believe it works.

The next day our group continued on its route firstly by plane closer to Sikkim and then via road through Sikkim and down to the southern border of Bhutan. Here we entered Bhutan through the border town (when Bhutanese describe it, you imagine cowboys and saloon bars) of Pheuntsohling. This large town offers an easy route between Bhutan and India to the south. Both populations increasingly move back and forth for shopping and work as the two countries develop closer links.

In Pheuntsohling there was a dividing wall between the two countries; on one side of it lay the enormity of India with its fast-track madness of motorbike horns and potholes. On the other lay the gentler rhythm of the Bhutanese way of living. There were school children walking in groups in their colourful, woven national dress, carrying packed lunches and chatting together on their way to lessons. No need to glance over their shoulders for fast approaching traffic. From Pheuntsohling we travelled north the six hours to Thimphu, the capital of Bhutan.

Karin and I were glued to the windows, living our first few moments in Bhutan with all our senses out on 'search' mode. We were finally there. It was real. Not a photo any longer; we were 110 per cent *in Bhutan*.

As a group we had a daily timetable and a responsibility not to miss the bus or get lost. Karin and I were determined to see and experience some of the daily Buddhist life and rituals of the country. Having just a few packed days of sightseeing available to us, we were worried we would somehow miss this. So, on our first morning in Thimphu, we got up early to visit the Memorial Chorten. This is a large, Tibetan-style stupa for locals to perform their daily circumambulations. A stupa (the Sanskrit word) or chorten (the Tibetan word) is a large structure with a base about 20 ft square and 20 ft high. Above this square base is a long spire, reaching up high into the sky. The exterior is plastered and painted white. In the centre of each of the four sides is a small inset shrine room. There are many such structures all over the Himalayas serving similar purposes. This is one of the larger stupas. In the Himalayas people often walk clockwise around temples or stupas such as these. Some traditions also walk anticlockwise but in Bhutan it's always clockwise, gently chanting or reflecting as you do.

We got there early in the morning and it was lovely to 'blend in' with all manner of Bhutanese people doing their soft walking-prayer. For a short while we became part of this ritual of gathering together in this sacred-everyday place. There were old women sitting, chatting, turning prayer wheels and cleaning brass butter lamp holders. There were school children in their neat striped uniforms and men in suits visiting the chorten before going off to the office. It seemed everyone was there and we became part of it. For both of us, who had never had the chance before to feel part of a totally Buddhist culture, it was amazing. To the people there perhaps it was nothing special, just normal; what they did every morning before their workday began. For us it was extraordinary in its quiet understanding.

As we left huge crowds of pigeons took off from their pecking on the ground and scattered in the air before relanding, seemingly, exactly where they had been.

I feel so at home…

Had I too grown wings, flown up and landed in my spot?

Walking back to meet the group, we were becoming familiar with the unique Bhutanese architecture of ornate wooden windows. Hand-painted representations of Himalayan birds, animals and phalluses adorned the sides of buildings. Some of them were real, some clearly mythological (including the phalluses!). This decoration connects back to a figure in Bhutanese history called Drukpa Kinley and, despite being told, I didn't quite get what the connections were between him and the house decoration. The older buildings have walls made of mud with white plaster showing within a dark timber frame. This can give these buildings a look of Tudor England with a decorated Himalayan twist.

On the streets, alongside the mothers and the monks, there was a large dog population in varied colours and states of health. I am not sure what the dog-to-person ratio is in Bhutan but I am betting on the dogs. Everyone says the dogs sleep all day and they do; under cars, in the middle of roads and sideways on the pavements, seemingly oblivious to the dangers of faster roads, gently snoring. They are the only ones who don't seem in the least bit worried by the pace of change in Bhutan's capital.

Thimphu is an increasingly modern Asian city but still small and it maintains much character despite the building of a large number of brightly coloured concrete buildings which stand alongside the older mud-built ones. It has a wide range of shops catering to a wide range of people: handicraft shops for tourists (chillips, as the Bhutanese tend to call anyone who is non-Bhutanese); everyday shops selling everything from melamine cups to roll mattresses and kids' Spider-Man pyjamas for the residents; and monk shops selling robes and jackets. It's a heady retail mix, particularly when pavements are narrow, the traffic close to your legs and you are doing your best to avoid open drains and sleeping dogs.

Travelling with Karin and Bridget made the trip very enjoyable but Bridget was still experiencing the tail end of a stomach bug so it was left to Karin and I to sample the Bhutanese whisky in the Thimphu hotel bar that evening. We were trying out K5, a whisky named in honour of the fifth and current king of Bhutan and it's an exceedingly friendly tipple. We had been told that the altitude would make drinking far more dangerous but Karin and I seemed to manage without any disasters. Many of the hotels had a lot of interior wood, sometimes highly varnished panelling. This one was of this variety. It gave you the feeling of drinking whisky in a shiny log cabin in the mountains.

We chatted about a full day in Bhutan which had included going to an art school where pupils learn traditional Buddhist arts such as thangka painting. These schools have been set up to ensure traditional arts and crafts survive as the country changes. Students learning the process of thangka painting begin by learning how to draw with pencil the precise shapes of Buddhist symbols and deities, forming them accurately with the guidance of a precisely measured pencil grid on which the forms are drawn. The next step is to master painting with a smooth line, not a hiccupy one (an interesting parallel to mind practices) and then to work on mastering the painting of faces, cloth and flowers. When the painting is finished, those with textile skills backed and set them in a border of beautiful material, giving them the capacity to be easily rolled up for travel. I was used to paintings set in wooden frames not soft, golden fabric with embroidered flower patterns.

Karin had visited the Institute of Traditional Medicine Services which was interesting from a yogic point of view in its interpretation of the many elements which determine the well-being of a whole human being.

Perhaps because I had left Oscar at home and because I was finally visiting a country I had wanted to visit for so long, I was pretty intense on the trip. I wanted to find out as much as I could and to dig down through the layers to see what was really there.

What is it here that's grabbing me so strongly?

At first I thought it might be Bhutanese culture or Buddhism, but I was soon to realise it is impossible to separate them. Buddhism has existed in Bhutan since at least the ninth century and it's hard to distinguish 'Bhutanese culture' from 'Buddhist thinking'. The close interweaving of culture and faith produces the feeling that Buddhist philosophy has touched all beings and aspects of this country. The most obvious modern example of this interweaving is the idea of considering the country's development through the lens of Gross National Happiness. This policy takes Buddhist principles and seeks to translate them in tangible ways to help the Bhutanese people steer their economic and cultural development.

In terms of Buddhism and in very general terms, the Eastern part of Bhutan has many people and buildings built under the Nyingma tradition of Himalayan Buddhism and inspired by the teachings of Guru Rinpoche (or Padmasambava) from India. The Western part of Bhutan has been more influenced by the development of Drukpa Kagyu Himalayan Buddhism, which was brought into Bhutan from Tibet by the Zhabdrung in the seventeenth century.

We were told to look out for statues representing both of these men and had already glimpsed dzongs, monasteries and lhakangs attributed to them. Dzongs are huge and beautiful fortress-like buildings with white walls and golden roofs which tend to feature on the cover of any book about Bhutan. They both perform a local government function and house a body of monks and so illustrate this indivisibility of culture, government and Buddhism in explicit physical form. Local people might visit dzongs over a land dispute or to ask the monks to do prayers for their sick relatives.

Lhakangs are local temples. Usually they are mud-built buildings, plastered and painted white with a thick band of orange painted seven-eighths up the sides, running under the roof. The centre of the roof is always topped with some gold decoration to signify its status as a lhakang and not just a regular farmhouse. They're often set in land with a slight wall to demarcate the area and usually there will be at least one tall, perhaps four foot high, brightly embossed prayer wheel outside which, when turned, causes a bell to ring, symbolising the sending of the prayers layered inside it, outwards.

Inside the lhakang there are mostly old wooden floorboards, perhaps with some concrete added later if there has been a concern that the butter lamps inside could cause a fire – it does happen. There is space in which to sit, to make offerings, to do prostrations and to look at the highly decorated walls showing the life of the Buddha as he lived in India, along with statues of other Himalayan teachers such as Milarepa, Guru Rinpoche, Zhabdrung and the representation of compassion, Chenrezig. Often these small temples are looked after by a family or an individual caretaker who lives close by. These individuals tend to the building and ensure its happy continuance for the benefit of the local community and visitors. By day two in Bhutan and three-quarters of the way through the trip, I had squeezed this information out of our patient guide Zara.

I asked our local Bhutanese guide more questions about Buddhist rituals and the way they impacted the lives of ordinary people in Bhutan. I was particularly interested to know what their rituals were when someone dies. Death is not a subject I am scared to discuss as we all have this in common and I find it fascinating to know how different cultures approach this most inevitable of human experiences. Dad had gone so quickly away from our house that day. I want to feel a little more prepared in the future. I want to have calmly considered this area more, for Mum at the very least. If I had not been able to do my very best for Dad I want to be of more help to her.

I was told that prayers are said near the person as they die and for up to ninety days afterwards. The body is preferably placed lying on their right side as shown in my statue of a reclining Buddha. Monks and nuns are brought in to perform prayers, make offerings and do all they can to guide this soul on its onward journey. The process of someone's awareness (we might call it 'soul') moving out of their body is seen as the most important moment of someone's life. It is viewed as the culmination of all that has gone before. The family and monastic practitioners left behind perform an important part in ensuring this soul carries on peacefully. I was reminded of how useless I felt after Dad died, clinging on to practical tasks. I needed to work in the old people's home. The ache

I had felt in the wish to carry on caring for someone had continued long after his death, wrapped inside a covering of grief. Ninety days – yes, it made sense to me – it was about the time I had worked at the old people's home for.

It seemed that, from a Buddhist point of view, all the actions, words and thoughts the dying person had experienced throughout their life would have a key bearing on what happened next. I think this is an oft-held belief in many faiths. What you do and say and think does have an impact. It is not invisible or unimportant. It matters to us all. Perhaps it is this which creates the seeds of our connected karma.

CHAPTER 19

A HIGH POINT

Too soon we left Thimphu to travel in the group bus to Punakha. The daily routine definitely had overtones of a school trip by now as everyone returned to their spot on the bus and leaned over the back of seats to talk to new friends. We all knew by now who was the photographer, who had the most encyclopaedic guidebook and who couldn't quite hear Zara as she talked, standing up, at the front of the bus.

Our first stop on the way to Punakha was at Dochula, a well-known tourist spot around forty minutes outside Thimphu. At an altitude of 3,050 m, it has stunning views of the Himalayan range standing up in a line sharp against the clear sky. Dochula is famous for its 108 small chortens, with the Himalayas as their backdrop. As we had seen at the Memorial Chorten in Thimphu, these structures are extremely important in the region. These chortens are plain white on the outside, but contain sacred texts and relics placed around a central pole, like a spinal cord. They are upright and rectangular in shape, as is often the case in Bhutan, and slightly taller than human height, with roofs of small grey slates.

Here again, as in Thimphu, Karin and I could see people doing their circumambulations around the chortens.

They walked at different paces and in different ways but always clockwise. Their movements were accompanied by the soft speaking of a mantra, such as the compassion mantra, *Om mani peme hung*, mumbled quietly as they walked. In their left hands hung their prayer beads, gently moving between their thumbs and first fingers. The beads were held up by the heart and swinging, from there, down in a loop close to the body. When these prayer bead strings aren't in use they're wound around the left wrist or hung around the neck.

A string of such prayer beads – a mala, – is usually made up of 108 beads, a sacred number in India and the Himalayas (hence Dochula's 108 chortens), with a larger central bead as an easy-to-feel start/end point. Such beads can be made from wood or seeds with a little looseness set between them to allow the easy movement of beads over fingers. They are a simple way to bring spiritual intention into daily life, easy to pick up when you have a quiet few minutes. Later we saw old women sitting on crates outside shops in Paro murmuring their mantras, beads smoothly running over the thumb and first finger, like stroking the back of a baby falling to sleep.

On that day most of the group walked around these chortens. Karin and I chose to walk the steps, built like an outside ladder, to the temple at the top of the hill. The view over the Himalayas from Dochula is famous and I felt I could giggle and leap into the sky, walking up the steep approach to the temple. The smell of incense spread out from two large, clay incense containers, their openings stuffed full with whole branches from juniper trees. We looked down on the chortens, placed with total accuracy in their neat circles, reminiscent of the structure of standing stones I had seen back home on childhood family trips to see 'history'.

Inside the temple there were wall paintings and, to the left side on entry, three large golden statues set on a wide, in-built ledge. In front of the statues was a table with a wide range of objects: candles, bowls of water, flowers, money and food. The wide range of offerings was designed to encourage the development of generosity and non-attachment in the mind. The statues were of three key Buddhist figures in Bhutan: the historical Buddha, Guru Rinpoche and the Zhabdrung. All three of these men existed as humans and achieved great understanding of the nature of the human mind. Their importance in the Buddhist world gives them a mythical status but they were real-life humans. They are seen to act, therefore, as inspiration to other humans seeking understanding.

To the left of these statues was a separate room where objects designed to placate local forces were placed. These side rooms speak of a more ancient culture of worshipping water and other elements and their personifications, a practice seen widely in ancient cultures of the world and one which probably pre-dates Buddhism in the Himalayas.

The rest of the room was fairly empty. There are no pews or lecterns in Buddhist temples as monastics sit on the floor on long, brightly coloured, woven rugs.

The main thing I noticed in the temple was a barefooted monk in the red robes and with the shaven head which is such a common sight in Bhutan. I noticed his barefootedness in particular given the high altitude and the fact that it was late October. I thought socks might be an idea.

How do you know when someone draws your attention, at a party, in a café or even inside a temple? I thought I saw a silver moon shining all around this monk's head like a dinner plate. *But how can that be?*

Perhaps it was the winter sunshine coming through the temple windows.

I went towards him and his wide, smiling face encouraged me. I said 'Hello' as the Bhutanese greeting of 'Kuzozangpo la' still evaded me at that point.

He answered and a powerful thing was suddenly set loose. I have heard the sound of an arrow pierce the air in an arc before landing, going straight to the point. It was like that.

What is this feeling?

His voice pulled me in. His way of talking was so full of kindness. I wanted to remain, to keep on talking to him.

We talked standing up, we talked sitting down, cross-legged, on the wooden floor of the temple.

I lost awareness of Karin's presence or indeed of whether there was anyone else there at all. I was surprised at the words that came out of my mouth. I found myself telling him, with apparently great sincerity, 'I want to be kind to people. I want to help people.' This was definitely not something I had said before to anyone and, even as I said it, I wondered where on earth it had come from.

Emma, what are you saying? Do you even really mean this?

Perhaps all the incense had somehow carried me away.

But still we carried on – it did not faze him to hear this honest statement from someone he had never met before. We talked about Kathmandu and the compassion mantra. I still could not make the sight of suffering and the practice of compassion add up. Saying this mantra would not bring those broken limbs back, it would not cause a child to stand up and look me in the eye – so was it really helping?

I mentioned the difficulty of finding time to practise meditation, what with a child and teaching yoga. I expected the monk to nod and empathise; surely that's what Buddhists did! Instead, he did not agree that these facts were to be defined as difficulties.

'Everyone is busy,' he said. 'You can make time.' It was an instruction, not a suggestion.

At some point I cried, such was the feeling of intense honesty welling up in me. After that I felt a little embarrassed and began to feel it was time to go. I got up and said goodbye to the monk.

I turned, leaving the temple rather dishevelled, still mildly snivelling. Outside and down the steps I found the rest of the group had gone.

Another waiting guide, seeing my lost hamster look, suggested they had probably gone to the nearby cafe at the Dochula Resort so I got a ride in a bus and went to find the rest of the group. Zara had indeed gone there to warm up.

All together again, we continued on to Punakha to see its famous ancient dzong and back, in a loop, to Thimphu.

Outside Thimphu we walked up to the monastery at Cherri, famous for offering monks the opportunity to do the traditional three-year, three-month, three-week, three-day retreat. Small retreat houses are scattered on the upper slopes around the main monastery. In here chosen monks would spend this time, occasionally seeing a visitor through the course of the three years in order to gain more teachings to practice or see a doctor if required. The main building of the monastery was built in the seventeenth century by Zhabdrung (he of one of the statues we had seen in the temple at Dochula). To reach the monastery you park near an arching wooden bridge which is more like a gallery in that it has struts on the sides and a wooden roof. Attached to this ornate bridge there are many prayer flags, their shapes throwing shadows into the fast-running white water of the river below.

The sound of the water is loud and drowns out all mental distraction as you walk across the wooden floor of the bridge. It's a powerful way to begin a walk to a spiritual place. Once over you continue walking upwards along a path which zigzags back and forth in order to make the mountain walk a little easier. We were there when it was quiet and I was able to go on ahead, hearing my footsteps walk a path so many people had trodden over the centuries.

Eventually I began to spy the distinctive wooden windows and stone walls of the monastery above me. I could see a red-robed monk sitting on a high ledge, looking out over the valley. He looked preoccupied. I was impressed, imagining him to be deep in reflection. As I got closer I saw he was doing something on a mobile phone. Alongside these small signs of modernity the monastery was majestic, situated giddily high up over the Thimphu valley. You could see trees like darts thrown down and a silvery river winding its way, silently, far below. In the main temple, monks were learning to play instruments made of copper and brass that looked like long hunting horns. Their sound was mournful and travelled right into your bones. It spoke to the preciousness and the impermanence of human life, sounds thrown upwards to move in the sky and around the mountain peaks.

Outside the main entrance a monk was standing and I smiled and moved to speak to him. I politely asked him how long he tended to meditate for – I meant every day. I was always interested to get exact goals and facts and figures! His answer was quiet and considered: 'A year, three years, maybe a lifetime.' *So not twenty minutes a day then* – I made a mental note.

These moments of teachings, these glimpses at the profundity and the weaving in of modernity within Buddhist practitioners in Bhutan were very fascinating to me. I was lucky the monks I had spoken to tended to have some grasp of English, a language that is learnt in all Bhutanese schools and makes Bhutan a more accessible place to visit than I had imagined from the magical glimpses I had seen in the travel guides.

Zara explained how Buddhist practitioners came in many different forms. I listened, taking it all in. Some were monks or nuns, some were not, and in between 'lay' and 'monastic' there were practitioners called 'Gomchens' who may have spent some time as a monastic but who were living more in the lay community. It seemed that monks, nuns, lamas and rinpoches might live in monasteries, dzongs, on retreat or in the community or a combination of all of them. It seemed surprisingly flexible. Rinpoches might be allowed the greatest degree of flexibility. In their status as confirmed rebirths of previous Buddhist teachers and meditators they are powerful figures in the landscape of Buddhism in Bhutan.

The majority of monks and nuns tend to live in a shared setting for at least a period of time even if they then leave to teach or retreat elsewhere. Financially they are dependent on the monastic institution for their shelter, food and education and this is mostly provided in a communal setting such as a monastery. Once a monk/nun has done some study, usually three years of Buddhist philosophy, they may be offered the guidance necessary to undertake a three-year retreat. This may be done alongside other retreatants or completely alone but will always occur in a setting strictly closed to the outside world. When completed, some of these monks will formally attain the title of 'lama'. The term 'lama' can be used more loosely in other countries but in Bhutan the completion of a three-year retreat is a requirement for formally gaining this rank. Zara was clear that there were many accomplished female practitioners in Bhutan but she had not yet met a Bhutanese woman with the title of 'lama'.

I relayed all this information to Karin over dinner that evening and, as budding female practitioners, we decided to try to visit a nunnery during the trip. Just to see…

We were granted this wish on our last two days in Bhutan. We had decided that, while the rest of the group flew to Calcutta, India, we would spend the extra time near Paro and fly on from there. Bridget went with the rest of the group to Calcutta as her friend David lived there, running a school for disabled children.

We discovered there was a nunnery outside Paro called Kila Ani Gompa. 'Kila' means 'a dagger' and 'ani gompa' means 'nunnery' in a loose sense. Ani loosely means nun and gompa is the verb to meditate. The dagger symbolises the energy and determination required to cut through the negative. 'Kila' could also have meant 'lung-retching walk at altitude up a steep hill and how on earth do you do this on a regular basis?' The start of the climb was already at high altitude and, regardless of the fact that we were both yoga teachers with lots of practice in breathing, we still felt as if our lungs were being squashed like tin foil.

Once there, in the cold of early November, we watched four nuns standing outside, putting their reddened hands in and out of a metal bowl of cold water. They were making objects called 'tormas', which are formed from coloured and softened butter, gently kneaded between their fingers to form strips, rounds or petal shapes. These shapes are then placed on wooden sticks of various lengths to make an object like a small totem pole to be placed on their shrine.

Karin and I went to sit in their little shrine room. We wanted to meditate. One of the resident nuns came in after a while and stayed standing with us. We spent a few moments in meditation. By that I mean that we were quiet, sitting cross-legged, hands resting in our laps, right hand in left hand, breathing.

As we finished I smiled up at the nun. She was standing, patiently waiting in her red robes.

'Were you meditating?' she asked, tentatively.

'Well, yes,' I said, glancing at Karin, somewhat surprised at the apparent tone of awe in her question.

'We don't get meditation teachings until we have done nine years of mantra,' she explained.

I digested this startling piece of information, remembering all those 'Meditation for Dummies' and 'Meditation in the Office' titles, spines showing, lined up in bookshops back home.

Has the West taken the East and turned it upside down?

I didn't want to cross-question a nun but was intrigued to know more about how meditation was viewed in the process of training as a monastic.

Karma, our local guide who was with us now for these extra sights in Bhutan, brought out a picnic lunch for us from a Mary Poppins-esque rucksack. We sat around the plastic table in the outdoor space between the kitchen, the shrine room and the living block. With his help we tried to understand a little of what it might be like to live at a nunnery on a mountain in Bhutan.

Such a life involved tending the shrine room, doing daily prayers, working to prepare and cook the communal food and reciting classical Tibetan texts by heart. It seemed half highly academic, half highly practical. As we had seen elsewhere, while all efforts are made to ensure the shrine room is as beautiful and inspiring as possible, the living conditions in the surrounding buildings were beyond basic. From the perspective of an Englishwoman used to central heating and a washing machine the practical questions of how you keep clean and washing your clothes quickly came to mind but it seemed a little impolite to ask a male guide where the nuns did their washing!

He explained that each nunnery has its own daily routine starting at 4 or 5 a.m., depending on how cold the season is. Their daily timetable, pinned up on the wall outside the shrine, showed little down time. I said so to our guide, amazed at how short the time was for the nuns to sleep.

'Oh yes, it's hard life. They are nuns.' He was stating facts.

'How do you think they manage then?' I was frowning, trying my best to understand.

'They have monastery inside them.'

'Ah yes,' I said, imagining the golden statues and beautiful shrines we had seen all over Bhutan replacing the wiggly shapes of organs.

Karin put on her grey woolly hat. I noticed the lights in the kitchen were going on and off and asked the guide if this was usual. He called over to one of the nuns, carrying a bowl of green beans. She came over and explained that electricity was available but temperamental. This on–off pattern repeated itself apparently, particularly in the evenings when light was needed. In the largely wooden building halfway up a mountain I tried to help.

'Maybe it's the fuse. Should we check the fuse box?'

'Oh no,' came the nun's jolly reply. 'It's the wind. When the wind blows – no electricity. When it stops – electricity. That naughty, naughty wind.'

I was left without words, unused to electricity which was so dependent on external conditions. I imagined the swaying wires, loose and dancing round the building, turning the electricity on and off. The realities of this tough communal living are still hard to grasp. It looked like a busy hive, only working because each participant is learning to think for the good of the whole and letting go of what no longer mattered.

I mulled these things over on our walk back. The simplicity and harshness.

How do they do it?

Heading down the mountain was easier on our breathing but even harder on our thigh muscles. Luckily we were having our final night at the most luxurious accommodation we had yet to encounter on the trip, a top-notch hotel named Zhiwa Ling. This title means 'place of peace' which was about all we were ready for after that walk.

Inside this hotel there was no more of the varnished wood panelling we had seen so much of. Instead, in came the joys of under-floor heating, richly carved wood and a stunning view of the famous Tiger's Nest Monastery high up in the hills. Karin and I had our moments of squealing like schoolgirls at the size of the rooms and the non-life threatening nature of the bathroom – we had had our fair share of scalded skin, frozen skin and moving loo seats on the trip.

We settled down for a very civilised dinner, feeling a growing reluctance to admit this was our final night in Bhutan. As we ate our meal in the restaurant, which culminated in homemade banana ice cream, I noticed a man with sandy hair and a name badge on his jacket. He was chatting to people as they had their dinner, passing from table to table. He looked friendly.

He came to ours and said, 'Hello, I am Brent the GM here; welcome to Zhiwa Ling. How is your dinner? Are you enjoying it?' This was all said with what sounded like an Australian accent.

Karin and I both enthused about how wonderful Bhutan was, how pampered we felt at the hotel and how sad we were to be leaving the next morning.

'So what brought you two ladies to Bhutan?' asked Brent.

'We wanted to see a Buddhist culture and had seen amazing pictures of Bhutan. We've both wanted to come for a long time.' Karin spoke for us both and I nodded, savouring the sweetness of banana on my tongue.

'I often hear that from guests here,' Brent confirmed. 'It's a special place. How do you two know each other back in the UK?'

'We both teach yoga. Emma is my yoga teacher, in fact.'

'Ah really, what's she like then, as a yoga teacher?' said Brent, sending me a smile.

'She's awesome. The best,' Karin replied with a big grin.

'Thanks, Karin, I will pay you back later!' I said, laughing. I added, 'What is a GM, if I can ask?'

'It means General Manager. Sorry, it's industry speak. I say it a lot! Look, I won't disturb you now but if you ladies would like to join me in the bar after your dinner maybe we can talk some more. Our yoga teacher here has just left and we may need one over the upcoming Christmas period. Sometimes people want to come here to avoid the festivities and do yoga.'

That was interesting to hear and Karin and I were always up for a Bhutanese whisky in a bar.

After dinner we moved across to the bar, chatting in front of a log fire with pictures of Bhutanese mythical tales painted on the walls around us. Brent, still on duty, drank soda water; we drank the whisky. He turned out to be a New Zealander who had been invited to run the hotel by its owner. He lived in a house provided close by to the hotel and was clearly passionate about Bhutan and committed to his job. His was easy company and when he floated the idea of me teaching yoga during the upcoming Christmas festivities, I did my best to convince him it made sense. Karin restated what a *great* yoga teacher I was and, chuckling, he said he would think about it. Walking back to our room and warmed by the whisky Karin and I were certain we had charmed him into the offer of a job.

The next morning Karin and I got up for our last breakfast in Bhutan. We were hoping the low-lying cloud hanging in the Paro valley would prevent our Druk Air flight from leaving, forcing us to remain captive in the Himalayas. But, sadly, it was not to be.

Brent came to say goodbye. He shook my hand in the spacious lobby and said, 'Looking forward to seeing you again.' It was an innocent enough comment but I was hoping against hope that it might actually mean, 'See you back in Bhutan soon, teaching yoga.' A night's sleep had convinced me that his offer was important and I definitely wanted to take him up on it.

CHAPTER 20

THE ROOTS OF THE TREE

Putting the future to one side, Karin and I flew to Delhi. It was hot and fast. Green-and-yellow motorbikes-cum-cars whizzed around corners on tyre edges, their horns sounding in air heavy with pollution and spice. We stayed in an airport hotel and hid from the speed and confusion, hoping to lengthen the quietness of Himalayan Mountains as long as possible.

From there we flew north and west back to our lives in England.

It was wonderful to see Oscar again and to appreciate so many things I had never noticed before: the smoothness of English roads and a loo which required no special procedure. I loved coming home to Whitstable, where I can smile at so many people I have known down the years. Whitstable itself was growing up. It had come to the attention of Londoners looking to escape to the sea at the weekends. The ironmongers had gone, although Whites of Kent with their extra-supportive lingerie displays remained. New people brought new needs, nice restaurants close to the beach, cafes and activities for kids. It was good. It felt more alive.

Bhutan didn't have the smell of the salty sea or great coffee shops with espresso machines but it had got me. Despite my love for my home town part of me was already missing Bhutan and ready to go back. Perhaps this feeling arose from spending time in a place where sacredness seems to so obviously touch everything. Everything was considered sacred; the mountains, books, rivers, land, trees and animals. I found this extraordinarily powerful. Oscar was precious to me, of course, my family too and a few prized possessions. But *sacred*? Was anything sacred to me?

Seeing the sky and mountains as sacred, *looking* in this way brought me great joy. It had been a long time since I'd felt that. I would probably have to reach right back into the sea and watch Dad in his red swimming trunks off Whitstable beach followed by the cold rub-a-dub-dub moment of getting towel dried on an English beach. It had been a long while since happiness felt so easy and natural. Bhutan was bringing it back to me from somewhere deep inside.

It had also allowed me to connect to a profound feeling of kindness both in meeting the monk at Dochula but also in seeing so many people and places dedicated to the mantra of compassion. This was, simply, very inspiring.

Back in England in 2011, I practised Buddhism with commitment, as the monk had instructed me. I remembered his voice so clearly. Sitting at home, as though in his presence, I began to feel our conversation was not over. I realised I definitely needed to go back. I needed to go back to Bhutan and find him. That feeling of *absolute certainty* reappeared with double-underlined, red pen, capital letters saying: 'GO – FIND THAT MONK.'

Via Skype to the hotel in Paro, I discussed with Brent the idea of returning to teach yoga for the Christmas period.

Mark was due to have Oscar that Christmas. I had already had one Christmas at home without Oscar and had missed him hugely so an alternative was highly appealing. Brent confirmed he did want a yoga teacher over the Christmas period. I said 'yes' and did not give him a second to rethink the idea.

Six weeks after leaving Bhutan, I got on a plane to Bangkok and then on to Paro. Paro is in the fertile west of Bhutan. It's where most visitors arrive into the country. It's an exciting way to enter as the small plane banks and then travels down the valley, seeming to brush the tops of conifers, and lands sharply next to haystacks and cows on a surprisingly short runway. It remains one of the world's most dangerous airports to land in. From the windows you can see Paro Dzong coming into view, and the winding river. The closeness is like being taken into the arms of your loved one.

The terminal building could be mistaken for a palace and new visitors delay passport control to stop and spend time photographing it. Brent picked me up there and we drove the twenty minutes to the Zhiwa Ling hotel where I was booked to teach yoga to both the guests and the hotel staff.

It was great to teach yoga to the Bhutanese staff, all of whom could sit easily on the floor, as is their daily habit in their own homes, and loved using their elbows to tip their colleagues over when in their yoga postures. They thought yoga was about having fun – a good thing for me to remember.

These lessons gave me a chance to get to know the staff and relax with them and I started taking staff lunch which was held around a large table in a back room. Brent and his management team would joke and eat and sort out work all in one go. There were about ten of us around the table and people would come and go according to duties and appetite. At the end of one of these lunches the head of housekeeping, Aum Sonam, and I were left musing over our milky tea and remains of some birthday cake.

'Aum' is the word for a mother in Dzongkha, the dominant language of Bhutan, and women who have had children are often addressed by this term, as if it's part of their name. I can't imagine English people calling women Mother Sandra or Mother Claire without their thinking I was casting them for *The Sound of Music* but, in Bhutan, it works.

Aum Sonam is in her early forties, with the wide face and high cheekbones showing her Tibetan heritage. She was always in the centre of stories at the lunch table and her presence always meant extra laughter. She made me feel very welcome and so it was easy to fast-track a friendship with her. Brent had mentioned that her father had recently died so I thought it would show kindness to express my sympathy. One thing led to another and, in typical Bhutanese style, a larger story emerged. It turned out that she was left a widow after her husband was killed in a car crash and so she had raised her son largely on her own. Following her husband's death she had had a boyfriend, Dorje, for eight years. Her father died, leaving her to take on the lion's share of caring for her elderly mother, and it was at this point that her boyfriend decided to leave her, taking a sizeable amount of her money with him.

She explained all this to me and I was appalled, coming from my viewpoint, expecting her to complain and take a long time to recover from such a betrayal. I recognise that I've only heard one side of things, however.

Instead she said, 'If he's not happy it's best he goes.'

'But how are you?' I asked. 'Are you not terribly upset that he has left you, especially at this difficult time?'

'Why make myself unhappy now? He is gone, it's in the past,' came her answer. It was hard to know what to say. I had not heard such a clear explanation of Buddhism in action despite reading so many books.

Rather stunned, we said a happy goodbye, and I wandered off to prepare a one-to-one yoga lesson for an American guest.

Christmas came and went in a gentle fashion. Brent had thought about arranging a small disco for guests but no one seemed very keen. Visitors in Bhutan at Christmas time are often there precisely to get away from Christmas and the Bhutanese do not celebrate Christmas; they're totally flummoxed when trees are deliberately cut down and brought indoors.

As it was quiet and no guests wanted to do yoga on Christmas Day Brent suggested we went on a hike. The sky was clear blue and we walked up a hillside to an old lhakang which was said to be built on a lake. We looked at the flooring as if expecting to see the lake appear beneath us but it didn't so we ate sandwiches outside, looking at a cloud drift into view and then dissolve back into the blue.

On the way down we had the great fortune to see a takin in the wild; way more exciting than seeing a turkey on a plate. The takin is thought to be a strange mixture of two other animals, probably a goat and an antelope. What we saw was a brown side flank showing like the side of a ship between the leaves, held up on stumpy legs. We stood still wondering what would happen next. The big brown side moved quietly back and the leaves closed around it. The takin was gone.

On Boxing Day I had time to organise my trip back to Dochula to go and find the monk.

I agreed with Brent to teach that day and the next and, with his help, arranged a car and driver for the next day – I did not want to tackle driving in Bhutan myself. Brent recommended a young Bhutanese man, Tshering (pronounced *Szarring*), to be my driver, as he knew he was a good driver with decent English.

So a day later we travelled the two hours from the wide valley of Paro to the higher altitude of Dochula, passing by Thimphu en route. Between Paro and Thimphu there's a decent road, following the river through a steep-sided valley for much of the way. As you pass you may see families picnicking along the riverside and above, on the slopes, tiny buildings designed for meditation retreat slightly stick out from stony valley slopes. These little buildings are usually set into rock where the front side has simply been placed over a cave-like space behind, with no obvious path to reach them. Inevitably your mind fills with the usual retreat questions of 'Where do you go to the loo exactly?' and 'How do you get food?' All the basic questions a human needs to know the answers to before they can relax and concentrate on something else.

That December it was cold driving to Dochula, the mountains a hazy blue above frosty rice paddies. Along the way I told Tshering the purpose of our trip. I explained that we were going to find a monk I had spoken to in the temple at Dochula a few weeks previously.

'Oh,' he said. 'What's his name?'

'I don't know,' I said.

'Well, what did he look like?'

'Yes… he was wearing red robes and he had a shaven head…' I ran dry of other details.

Tshering clearly wondered about me at this point. Another unfathomable tourist! It struck me that I couldn't really remember what the monk looked like. I had no photo. I couldn't, in fact, remember if he was tall or short. What I did know was his voice. This I was sure of. This I would always be able to recognise.

Feeling sweat gathering in my armpits, we continued. I explained to Tshering that I had formally been a Buddhist for about ten years and had mainly practised the meditations of compassion. I told him that speaking to this monk in October had been very helpful for my understanding and I felt a strong wish to find him again and talk more. Tshering began to warm to the adventure and, as we parked the car at Dochula in front of the circles of chortens, we were both keen to see how this story would turn out.

I strode determinedly up the monastery steps, past the incense holders, with the forwardness and anxiety of a Western woman attempting a blind date with a monk…which the monk knew nothing about.

Tshering came with me, wearing his vertically striped grey gho, the national dress for a man in Bhutan. His dark hair was slicked back, smooth, as is the fashion with young

Bhutanese men. He was slight in body yet did not seem to feel the cold.

We reached the large outer doors of the temple with their ornate brass rings. I took a deep breath.

Inside everything was the same, and a tall monk was standing with his back to me; it was all there: the red robes, the shaven head and the bare feet.

Tshering leaned towards me. 'Madam, is it him?'

I walked to the right side and the monk turned round in greeting.

I don't understand. How can it not be him? Where can he be?

'No. No, it's *not* him,' I answered with obvious disappointment.

Perhaps I had read too many meditation books and presumed the monk would somehow know I was coming back to find him. I checked and checked but no matter how hard I looked at this monk, I could not make him into *my* monk. It was definitely December, not October.

This monk had little English but luckily Tshering stepped in to help and translated back to me. I was told that the monk who had been there in October was now in retreat, for three years, near Punakha.

A big, empty pause occupied my head as if someone had blown air in through my ear.

Suddenly the long journey from England to Bangkok, from Bangkok to Paro, from Paro to Dochula and up the stairs ran speedily through my mind. It had simply not occurred to me that it would stop here, like this.

'Gone? On retreat? For *three* years?' I heard myself say.

Deflated, we left, walking slowly and silently back down the steps towards the 108 chortens.

We drove to the same Dochula Resort cafe.

Now I noticed how cold the air really was. It was December and we were over 3,000 m up, far away from my usual sea level. Inside the cafe Tshering and I stood close to a large, metal wood burner shaped like a standing iron barrel. Lying on the top of its lid were smooth, round stones which we picked up and held between our hands for warmth. We had unusual-tasting coffee and some chocolate bourbon biscuits. There was not much to say.

I felt lost in Bhutan and sorely lacking a plan B.

I looked round aimlessly, noting the pictures of Bhutan's Royal Family that hung from the walls. The tables in the cafe were simple and highly varnished, laid with thin, pink paper napkins curled up in small glasses, ready to be used.

Tshering's phone rang – mobile phones are common in Bhutan. As I had seen at Cherri both lay and monastic people often have mobile phones. Bhutan is a country where fixed-line phone development has been skipped and they've jumped straight to mobile. As Tshering was talking in Dzongkha I had no clue what was being said.

My nose felt cold as I waited, stamping my feet a little to help my blood circulate.

Tshering put down the phone and turned to me. 'That was the monk from the temple. He knows who you are looking for.' His voice was excited. 'It's not a monk, it's a *lama*. You met the Lama of this temple.'

'Oh,' I said, taking it all in.

'He remembers you too and, yes, he would like to meet you again. Right now he is in his home village doing rituals but we have his number and you can call him there.'

We were both smiling now. Smiling that this was not in fact The End.

Tshering seemed impressed that this lama had remembered me but I figured there weren't many Western women who had sat on the floor with him and cried. But who knows? Anything was possible in this land of clouds and ancient myths.

So now I had to call a monk – who was in fact a lama – who was doing rituals, whose face I couldn't remember with sketchy English – and make plans to meet up.

All this had to be arranged over a mobile phone pressed to my ear in a hand warmed by a stone worn smooth by the river below. I took a moment to collect myself and then asked Tshering for his phone.

Luckily, when I called him, the Lama just told me what would happen, which was a relief; the remains of the corporate woman in me had assumed I would have to take responsibility for Absolutely Everything. But no, he told me he would come to Paro to meet me on 31 December. I had planned to have a little champagne and frivolity with Brent on 31 December, it being New Year's Eve, but that plan was shelved.

I had a lama coming to see me.

CHAPTER 21

THE LAMA

Sitting in the hotel lobby on New Year's Eve I was waiting for the Lama to arrive.

The front door of the hotel seemed a long way away from where I was sitting. I hoped I would recognise him. My short-sightedness encouraged me to put my glasses on but my fear that they would fall off my nose as I greeted him held me back.

What am I going to say? Suddenly I got cold feet, wondering why on earth I had felt so sure I needed to talk to him again. *What exactly is it that I so badly need to talk to him about?* I couldn't remember any more. I needed a plan to hang on to but I didn't have one.

There was a pause and then the double doors opened and in came a beaming man with a dark orange cloth over his left shoulder, a red jacket and monks' robes. He was here.

Without thinking, I was filled with courage. I went over to greet him, finding tears coming once again, so powerful was the impact of being near this person.

When you see someone again after the longest time, when you thought you had lost them and then they are *there* in front of you, it feels natural to cry. Wouldn't you?

What squaring of a circle was this? If there had been a musical backdrop it would have involved someone humming Lennon's 'Instant Karma', describing something which is capable of knocking you off your feet. The possibility of a force which allows you to recognise places and people that you were certain, up until then, that you had never seen before.

Coming through a door was a Bhutanese monk who had a limited grasp of English, so why did I feel like the sun had just come out?

I presented him with the long white silken scarf that is a traditional greeting in Himalayan countries. Slightly bowing, I held it out like a silken hammock between my hands, offering it to him.

He took it and returned the greeting by placing the silken scarf around my neck.

We walked over to sit down on the lobby chairs and Brent came to greet him. I was relieved to have the pressure taken off with the addition of a third party. We all had tea and biscuits and tried to have a fluid conversation in English – not easy, but we all did our best.

I can remember little of the content of the conversation now except that what I *felt* and what I *knew* were markedly different. I *felt* absolute joy at being near this person and hearing him. However, I *knew* practically nothing about him, not even his name at this stage. Feeling complete, spontaneous devotion to someone it's not easy to communicate with is interesting. Maybe it's a little like looking at the miracle of your newborn child before you.

I found out that he had once left Bhutan for a Buddhist event in Nepal but, besides that, had a limited knowledge of the world outside Bhutan. It was evident he had not had much experience of discussing suffering with Westerners and perhaps he had an innocent idea that, once out of poverty, life would be quite easy. Perhaps we were both going to learn something from each other.

After our tea he left to rest in his room – he was staying in the hotel too. It is often courteous to allow a lama to stay in a hotel as a guest; this is seen as polite and also an auspicious event. We watched him walk up the stairs in his robes and brown shoes, carrying his small overnight bag. There was something very deliberate and considered about him.

Once out of sight Brent and I sat down again.

'So what do you think?' I asked.

'Yes, he seems good, simple; a proper practitioner,' was Brent's assessment.

'He is great, isn't he? I just wish it was a *little* easier to talk to each other in English,' I had to admit with a grin.

'You seemed to do OK. Don't worry,' he reassured me. 'So what's the plan now then? How's your New Year's Eve shaping up?' he said, changing the subject.

'After his rest he said to meet up for supper. Beyond that I have no idea.' I smiled, relaxing. 'Not sure I'll be partying though.'

'OK but hopefully you can squeeze in one glass of champagne after that. Bella and a couple of her friends are popping by about ten.'

It was nice to have the invite to join in with other expats working in Bhutan but my mind was already thinking up conversational subjects for later. I felt nervous about the possibility of awkward pauses over a supper with a Bhutanese lama.

At seven, Lama returned to meet me in the lobby and we had our supper together in the hotel restaurant, at the same table Karin and I had sat at a few weeks earlier. There was not a lot of spoken conversation.

Towards the end of the meal he announced, 'OK, I will see you in the morning, in the shrine room at six.'

'OK, great.'

'Goodnight then,' he said, standing up.

I followed his cue and we walked out of the restaurant.

Brent was by the reception desk and came over to us. 'All OK, Lama, everything alright with your room?'

'Yes, yes; very nice thank you. Now I am saying goodnight.' He definitely didn't waste his words.

We both said goodnight to him and watched his measured steps as he walked back towards the wide staircase.

'Done?' said Brent, turning to me. 'Ready for some champagne?'

'Gosh, well, I'm certainly ready for something,' I said, laughing. 'I have never had a meal with a lama before!'

We sat down in the comfy sofas of the hotel bar, in front of the open fire.

'So?' said Brent.

'Yes, no, everything is fine,' said I, covering all options as you do when you're not really paying attention. 'He told me to meet him in the shrine room at 6. I wonder what that means.' I was thinking out loud.

'Well, you won't have to wait long to find out. Come on, Bella and Richard are nearly here. Let's have a drink to celebrate the start of a new year.'

Lying in bed later, I spent the final night of 2011 anxiously checking the clock to make sure I had not missed my 5.40 alarm call. Waking every couple of hours, excited and waiting to find out what was going to happen next, time passed over into the first day of 2012.

I got up and went to sit on one of the square, firm cushions of patterned wool in the shrine room. I had with me my compassion prayers, a notebook and no clue of what was to happen next.

It's unusual for a hotel to have its own shrine room but Zhiwa Ling offered this truly five-star accessory. The shrine room was very warm and a loud clock ticked. The statues sat quietly. They had seen it all before.

I heard some slow, deliberate steps. The Lama appeared, smiling freely, and after lighting three butter lamps on the shrine, he sat down on a cushion next to me. He taught me about the compassion prayers for an hour and a half with a fair number of hand gestures and adjustments for English.

In this compassion practice it is necessary to imagine the sacred sound syllables of compassion – *Om mani peme hung* creating a circle which moves in your heart centre.

First you imagine a moon disc set horizontally in the centre of your chest and the six individual sounds of the mantra expressed in visual form and standing upright and moving round like a slowly spinning top. It is an inward version of what your left hand is doing as the mala beads circle round, touched by your thumb and first finger. Gently your mouth will say the sounds. Action, speech and mind together in compassion.

OM MA NI PE ME HUNG are the six syllables seen to be the concentrated expression of compassion.

As he talked it all through I wrote lots of notes and tried to both keep up and take time to enjoy this new experience of sitting next to such an experienced meditator.

Once we had covered my remaining questions Lama said he needed to do 'smoke offerings now' and told me to practice. I tidied up the rectangular prayers before me and quietly recited the prayers and practiced the visualisations with my mala beads.

We sat like this, side by side, in the shrine room. I didn't want to peer at what he was doing so I don't know exactly what he was up to. At the end he turned to me and, leaning over, took the mala beads I had been using.

'These no good,' he said. He took the deep brown prayer beads wrapped around his left wrist and handed them to me. 'These better. They will charge you a lot if you buy. For me, easy.'

This may have sounded like Tarzan talking to Jane but it decided things. That was that. He was to be my teacher and I was to be his student.

CHAPTER 22

SUNSHINING

I knew I had met someone who was to be important to me but beyond that I had no idea of what the future would hold.

Lama left after breakfast. We said goodbye at the hotel doors and then I went to the reception desk, resting my elbow on its surface. I asked the receptionist to slowly pronounce his name to me. It can take a while to grasp someone's name when it's spoken to you, quickly, in Dzongkha. She said he was Lama Nima Tshering. This means 'Teacher Sun Long-Lasting'. I already knew his address: the Temple at Dochula, near Thimpu, Bhutan. He had given me a phone number which he explained *might* work for calls but would not work for texts and would always depend on whether reception was possible that day at this high altitude.

I returned to England a few days later and continued with the mix-and-match lifestyle of a mum/yoga teacher/Buddhist practitioner. It was the type of maths I liked: a combination of.

'Osc, do you need a packed lunch?' I would call up to him as he searched out a crucial Lego figure in his bedroom.

+ 'OK, let's start by lying down. Concentrate on feeling your body fully breathe out. Feel the ground and let go of all the moments of today up to the point of being *here* in class now,' I would speak calmly as my yoga students rested on the floor around me.

+ *May all beings have happiness and the cause of happiness, may all beings be free of suffering and the causes of suffering.* I would pray and reflect on these words as one of my daily tasks given to me by Lama as another part of learning compassion.

= I was much happier.

It might sound like I was back to juggling patterns of old but it didn't feel like that any more. It felt like the scattered pieces were beginning to finally connect.

In March 2012 I took Oscar on his first visit to the Kagyu Samye Ling monastery in Scotland where I formally became a Buddhist years earlier. Oscar sat on my lap in the shrine room as afternoon prayers with drums and cymbals filled the space. I thought he would get twitchy but instead he comfortably sat and went to sleep. I felt him lying in my lap as the rhythm of the prayers developed and went deeper. Afterwards we went to the Buddhist shop close to the temple. Oscar tried out all the hand-held prayer wheels and decided he needed one. We went to the Tibetan tearooms next door. Oscar was happily occupied with his new prayer wheel, trying to get it to turn smoothly and in a clockwise direction in his small hand. He liked a challenge even at the age of five!

With no one else around and Oscar happy, I decided to call Lama. I had not had the courage to call him yet and I was not sure what I wanted to say anyway. Now I felt I really wanted to. I dialled the long number and waited, hearing a funny, sing-songy tune from the other end – a ring tone in Dzongkha perhaps?

'Hello' came the faraway voice. Again the tone was very matter of fact.

'Hello, Lama. It's Emma, your student here in England,' I said, hoping it was not too long a sentence for his fragile English.

'Oh, nice to know that. How are you?' The words were perfect; it was just that their rhythm went up and down like a slalom skier from the Himalayas and into my ear.

'Yes, yes, I'm fine, Lama,' I said, relieved it was possible to understand each other across the phone. 'I wanted to thank you, Lama, for all your teachings and for my mala beads. I cannot thank you enough.'

'No bother, no bother.'

Then I found myself saying with a slow pause, 'Lama, you are in my heart.' I said it simply because I thought he truly was there, in my heart. Talking to him had made this feeling arise but, even as I said it, I worried it sounded weird, like I had a crush on a monk.

'Thank you,' he said quietly with a stillness which told me it was fine. He had understood.

Since that time I have asked Lama what the title of 'lama' means. 'It is the one who teaches you, guides you to the Enlightened,' was his exact reply. In books you're more likely to read that 'lama' means 'highest teacher', a rough equivalent to the word 'guru' in yoga terms.

'Enlightenment' is a word frequently heard in Bhutan and in any teachings of a yogic or Buddhist nature. It's a state of being of complete wisdom, described as a mental state of complete light beyond the apparent limitations of a physical body. A state of being it's impossible to describe in a book! And having not reached it, I am ill-equipped to even hazard at a true definition; I am only passing on what I have been told, what I have read. Perhaps it is all only possible with an enormous jump of faith or a dedicated teacher.

In the Himalayan tradition spending time moving towards this state is seen as a highly meaningful way to spend a human life. In monastic robes it is my job description.

Himalayan teachings come from the Mahayana tradition of Buddhism which has strong links back to the development of Indian philosophy in ancient universities such as Nalanda, long after the life and times of Sakyamuni Buddha, who lived in the sixth century before the Common Era.

As this Buddhist approach spread outwards from India it developed, often incorporating local pre-existing traditions, as in Bhutan. However, one constant was the emphasis placed on compassion as the motivation behind practice and as essential in the process of transformation to realising an Enlightened mind.

I was Lama's student from afar for seven months, practising the compassion prayers according to his Christmas instructions, until I returned to see him in July 2012. I was en route to visit a nunnery in Bumthang in the central valleys of Bhutan. I had been asked by a friend of Brent's in Bhutan to help the nuns with their yoga, which was the 5 a.m. activity in their daily programme. Word had got round that I was a good yoga teacher and seriously interested in Buddhism and this fitted the description of who they were looking for to reinspire the nuns in their daily practice.

Once again Tshering was my driver and friend. The drive from Paro to Bumthang was significant, as was my car sickness through the valleys and winding mountain roads for nearly six hours. Along the way we planned to stop to see Lama again. Although Tshering did not know it, I had in my mind a plan for our next meeting. I had decided to ask Lama to shave my head.

The idea of cutting my hair off was not a big deal for me. I'd done it before, aged twenty-two. I'd had no religious reason for doing it back then – it was just an impulse from somewhere which happened to feel right. I had liked the freedom it gave then and I still do. The Bhutanese call it having a 'fresh head' and this is a good description. For a Buddhist a shaven head has great significance. It's a sign of the renunciation of outward concerns and desires. It's most commonly done by practitioners who are following, or are interested in following, monastic vows.

The three of us sat down at Lama's little home by the temple: me, Lama and Tshering, who was helping translate. After discussing various points of dharma (Buddhist teachings), I paused and said I had something to ask of him. It suddenly occurred to me that the request might break some kind of vow Lama had taken – maybe he was not allowed to touch a female's head. I just didn't know.

I wasn't sure how to put it so I just said, 'Lama la, I would like hair like yours.' I was careful to use the respectful adjunct of 'la' in making the request.

Lama looked a little confused.

Tshering wondered what he had to translate and asked me to clarify what it was I was asking for.

I said slowly and firmly that I would like Lama to cut my hair off and consider it an offering to him as my teacher. I gestured using two fingers as scissors around my head to illustrate the point.

Lama looked unmoved; Tshering looked a little worried.

Tshering said, 'No, no, it's not necessary. If you like, Lama can just take a little bit from your hair.' He gestured as if to pull the crown of his head up with string.

But I wished Lama to shave my whole head and I said so again. Just a few strands were not enough.

Luckily Lama seemed quite content with the request and said, 'Fine, fine.'

Tshering then relaxed, seeing all was turning out well.

We discussed the logistics. Lama needed to check which day would be the most auspicious for this event. To get the right day was important. He looked through a horizontal script with wheels on the front of it and decided on the best day. He said he would go to his monk friend in Thimphu to pick up the hair clippers. I said it would be nice to do it outside. Lama looked at me and gently pointed out that we would need electricity for the clippers.

On the right day, in the afternoon, sitting down inside, on a rattan chair, I bent my neck forwards and Lama began to shave my head. I rested a sheet of handmade Bhutanese paper on my lap and Lama dropped my hair on to it. I could feel he was concentrating, wanting to do it right. I had an awkward bump on the top of my head to negotiate with the clippers.

I had long blondish hair which people, later, told me had been rather nice. As my hair fell it felt light and fluffy. Tshering folded it up in the natural paper and I reached back to feel the skin on the back of my neck and around my scalp. My head felt freed like a bell taken out of its wrapping, ready to make its first clear sound.

*Ah…*I could feel myself take a long breath out.

We drove to a bridge, which was also fairly light and fluffy. We stood in the middle where it sagged a little and all swayed with it, rocked gently by the breeze. Lama opened the paper packet over the side and my hair floated down into the water. We moved to the other side but we could not see it. It had already gone, disappearing back to Thimphu.

There was no staircase of clouds to walk up. There was no rainbow to sit on. There was just me and Lama and Tshering looking down at the water below. Around us the gentle flap of prayer flags reminded me that we were standing together on a bridge in Bhutan. The Himalayas were behind us and India far in front of us. Space was huge and I felt it was possible to jump through it, weightless, with the ease of a butterfly resting on flower after flower.

We drove back to Lama's house for tea. I left Lama to chat to Tshering as they sat together in the front. At his house I explained to Lama that my shaved head might have to be a one-off occurrence as if Oscar did not feel comfortable with seeing his mother in this way, then I would need to grow it back. Lama understood. He gave me a pair of loose, saffron trousers used for Tibetan yoga and prostration practice and we left to travel the further hours to reach the central region of Bhutan.

On the long journey, Tshering and I talked about many things. Lama had given me a mantra to learn called the 100-syllable mantra. I began to practise it in the car, learning it line by line, with about eight syllables in each grouping. The 100 syllables are largely in Sanskrit, the honorific language of yoga, rather than in Tibetan as so many prayers and mantras tend to be in the Himalayan region. A mantra such as *Om mani peme hung* is made up of six syllables so mastering a whole 100 such sounds was going to require some mental application!

Between quiet repetitions, sitting in the front seat next to Tshering, he asked me if Lama was my 'Tsa Wai Lama'. This translates as your 'root lama'. I had not really thought about it but, 'Yes,' I said, I thought he was. According to Himalayan thinking your root teacher is the teacher you have an existing connection with, formed over time before this particular life. It is considered very good fortune to find them again.

I remembered sitting in earth, by a long tree root disappearing into the ground, a silver moon shining in the night sky.

Visually I was now a curious mix of West and East. I had a shaven head but was still wearing a silver necklace and a mother-of-pearl ring on my ring finger. I had simple sandals and plain Western clothes but no robes. Seeing a shaved head above regular clothes, someone might have wondered if I was recovering from chemotherapy. It was perhaps a little strange but I was happy trying out having one foot in the East and one in the West.

I spent a week with the ninety-six nuns living in the large ani gompa, or nunnery, in Bumthang. Their buildings formed a quadrant with an open courtyard where the nuns occasionally hit a badminton shuttlecock to each other as they ran around in robes, a way of letting off steam from their daily prayers and study perhaps.

Each day I planned a long lesson for them which they did in their communal hall under the shrine room on the south wall of the quadrant. The nunnery had brought in the services of a local Bhutanese woman, Dawa, to act as translator for the nuns who didn't have so much English. She was also keen to do the yoga though so often had to come up from a forward bend to call out a Dzongkha translation before dipping back down again.

Away from male gazes the nuns changed into loose trousers for the lessons. At first they were a little reticent but soon started to get louder, trying postures and chatting with their neighbouring nun or groaning like any yoga student does occasionally.

I had been asked to look out for potential yoga students capable of leading or teaching others when I left so towards the end of the week I divided everyone into groups with allocated leaders as part of this process. These leaders then had to work with their groups to draw a set of yoga postures based on what they had learnt in the week with a view to doing these practices once I was gone.

It was easy to see the camaraderie that existed between the nuns, the feeling of a large family with a clear purpose. It was nice to be part of it if only for a short while. Towards the end of my stay Tshering mentioned to them that I had a child. They were so interested to see and I was able to show them a photo of Oscar on my phone. They crowded round looking.

'So nice, so nice,' they repeated, talking back in Dzongkha to the nuns behind them to explain what was going on. I was aware that all of these young nuns had either probably never had a child or probably never will. It was a poignant moment for lots of reasons as they repeated a soft 'ah' sound in their throats.

After a week they had made great progress and I was sorry to leave but my mum duties back in England were calling. As I left, one of the older nuns presented me with a short, red piece of material, like a simple shawl, which is used by novice nuns. I was really touched by this kindness. Along with the saffron-coloured loose trousers from Lama, I had the beginnings of a new wardrobe. I bought a simple red sleeveless top on the way back through Thimpu and put my fitted black leggings further down in my case. It was a definite improvement on the slightly awkward combination of a shaved head and jeans; now the head and the body were starting to work together.

On the way back to Paro we stopped once again to see Lama at Dochula. I had been practising the 100-syllable mantra he had told me to learn and I wanted to speak it to him before it fell out of my brain as I thought it surely must do.

We stopped at his house and, after tea sitting on the floor, Tshering left me to speak to Lama. I told him I had an offering for him and, closing my eyes to concentrate, recited the 100-syllable mantra to him as well as I could. He sat quietly for a moment after and I thought he made a gentle nod.

We continued on to Paro and I got ready to leave Bhutan once more after another short but concentrated trip, I decided I would continue to wear my new coloured clothes on my journey back home to England. I took other Western clothes in my hand luggage, just in case: my white jeans, a silver belt and my crossover purple L. K. Bennett top. I thought about nipping into the plane toilet to change as we approached landing but decided not to. No, I would arrive in England exactly as I had left Bhutan.

Walking through the arrivals terminal at Heathrow, I was greeted with a full-force running leap from an excited Oscar. Mark had kindly brought him to the airport and I would take Oscar back home with me from there.

After a huge, long hug, I asked Oscar, 'What do you think, Osc? My hair – is it OK?'

'Fine, Mummy,' he said, hugging me again.

'And the funny yellow trousers?' I enquired, squeezing him super tight.

'Fine, Mummy,' he repeated, laughing happily.

'OK. Well, if it's OK with you, I'll stay like this then.' I was a bit taken aback at his certainty. 'Love you, Oscar.'

'I love you, Mummy.'

He had freckles, I had dimples. We knew we were a great team.

EVERY FLOWER HAS A SEED

Maybe every time you let something go,

a flower grows.

Imagine that.

The perfume and the honey.

CHAPTER 23

LEARNING FROM A LAMA

So that was that. The no-hair hairstyle was staying. I went shopping for my own set of clippers.

Although I looked very different from the other mums at the school gate I felt much more content. It felt so good to be freed from the habit of constantly checking my external appearance; to make sure it was attractive and pleasing to the eye. Some of the mums were curious as to why I now had no hair but soon it became the norm and no one asked; we were all mums getting on with getting our daily jobs done. Oscar said I looked the happiest mum and if anyone asked he just told them to look up who the Dalai Lama was!

Along with the hair I was wearing the loose saffron trousers Lama had given me, the red wrap and a simple sleeveless red shirt. I was ready to let a lot of past habits go, not just outer garments and habits of make-up, hairbrushes and a multitude of accessories.

It felt like a true bid for freedom. At last.

Oscar was six and I was forty-six, and I was ready.

Alcohol and sex were left behind. I was tired of old habits. *I* had been tough on *me* all of my life. I had tried and tried and not relaxed. I had looked for happiness – in painting, in money, in relationships. I had looked outwards and never found it.

In particular I knew I no longer wanted to go to a wedding or a party and spend half my time looking round for The One, for someone to complete me. I wanted to stop all the mental straining and give in to being a simple, human being who might be capable of the deep kindness I had seen in my teacher.

I was ready to live differently. I had an 'aha' moment as clarity emerged about what it was for me to be a human being, of the values I wished to guide me through the rest of my life. Pratyahara, my mind was moving inward. Prat-Y-A-Ha-Raaaaaaaaaaa. It was a long time since I had first heard this word above the soft turning of waves on an Australian beach but now its memory was coming back to me.

Teaching yoga remained an essential part of living in the West where I was not under the support of a nunnery as I would have been in Bhutan. Luckily I had no mortgage by this stage (thank you, banking) and Mark was a supportive co-parent – even so teaching remained a practical necessity. While running my life was also far cheaper (gone were the trips to hairdressers, clothes shops and so on), returning to Bhutan for future teachings required funds.

Fortunately, I enjoyed teaching. The nature of the classes was changing, perhaps reflecting my own internal changes. It too had slowed and calmed and contained a large dose of humour which was useful in keeping my students relaxed. I began to weave aspects of meditation and philosophy into the lessons, using the teachings I had gained to help my own students survive the pressures of daily life in the West. I felt a profound sense of care for my students and a deeper trust began to grow between us. They talked to me more openly than before and I tried my best to be of help.

In yoga classes my teaching methods were friendly, humorous and designed to place students at ease. They were different from the way of learning in Bhutan with Lama.

The teachings he gave me were quite business-like in style. They didn't include much small talk or elaboration but were pithy and sutra-like. This may also be due to the fact that, in the beginning, we had to pull words out from a mixture of languages, resorting to dictionaries on his part and diagrams and exaggerated facial expressions on mine. I found that when chit-chat is taken away, conversations don't take that long.

If Lama and I were to spend two whole days together, we would very soon run out of conversation. His job is not to chat about the weather but to give me precise, useful instructions in developing an understanding of a Buddhist view and experiencing mental stability and insight. Usually, as our teachings end, he tells me, 'Right. Now it's time for you to take some rest.' That's a dismissal in Lama speak. When he's finished, he's finished. He doesn't just chat. Once this form of teaching led to us both falling asleep at the end of a session. Once it led to an excruciatingly long supper when he had nothing left to say and I felt clammy with nerves as an expected social event lacked any social aspect. We had done our teachings earlier in the day so what else was there left to say? Now my job is to practice, to seek to understand and fully become what I have learnt from my lessons with Lama.

Lama tells me off if I appear to be showing any whiff of getting attached to him. He isn't interested in having a groupie.

This is good. It gives me certainty that his motivations for teaching me are true.

From a Western background my habit is to ask questions. To the Bhutanese I can be seen as highly inquisitive, a quality they're not too sure of at first. 'You are always asking questions, questions' is a comment I have had from many of my Bhutanese friends. Bhutanese are often quite private about things and it's easy for a Westerner's enthusiasm to understand to come across as intrusive probing. You have to learn these things as you go along.

Lama would chuckle and hold his head. 'You drive me crazy with your questions.'

I would ask him if he had any more students now.

'No, no, I can't cope with more questions – you give me enough already.'

Lama gives me a few small sentences to remember. If I could just remember to remember these small things all the time I would have made more progress by now. The thing is, one doesn't always remember. As our interest in 'mindfulness' demonstrates, we're beginning to understand how easy it is to revert to being a bee in a jar; a fall-back of running on mental habits we mistake for our true selves. Can you see why yogic texts describe life as a bee trapped in a glass vase – and why finding a way out is called freedom?

The majority of Lama's pithy teachings have taken place in his little house, behind the Temple, at Dochula. I say his house but it's not owned by him. He merely stays there while his role is to look after this temple. It's a traditionally built house made of a timber frame filled with mud-packed walls. You enter it up some small steps, which means the ground floor of the building is above the ground level. The front door is in the centre of the building. A thick piece of material is hung behind the door so you have to lift this to one side and duck under. You enter directly into the small 'sitting room', which is a room with not a lot in it, and a permanent chill due to its lack of heating. To the right is a little corridor kitchen with a side room off it for another monk/attendant and then, through the kitchen, is a basic bathroom with a constantly wet floor.

To the left of the 'zen' sitting room is Lama's room, which is where we sit. His room is around eight foot by nine foot. We often sit by his plug-in heater as this is the only heating in the building and the wooden windows allow draughts in.

There is a shrine on the left with golden offering bowls set on a ledge in front and Buddhist texts neatly stacked to the right and above. On the opposite wall are cushions and extra bed covers piled up. On the right wall is Lama's set-in wooden bed, like a bunk bed with no legs. His bed has a blanket and a pillow covered with a towel – I think he uses this arrangement so he doesn't need to wash the pillowcase, just this small head towel. Behind the bed are many books and pictures and photos of teachers and friends.

In front of the bed is a small prayer table of the type typically seen in monasteries. The table is the perfect height for someone sitting on the ground. Monastic practitioners should sit or lie low down whenever possible as a clear symbol of humility and connection to practice. The usual objects of practice – prayer books, bells, rice and so on – are placed on the table.

Usually Lama sits on top of his low bed, wearing his robes, referring to textbooks to the side of him and on his little table, as I bring my questions to him. He gives me a similar table, bringing it in from the sitting room so that I can sit to the side of him with my books and questions. Sitting like this together we make the shape of an 'L'.

Lama has a few personal objects in his room. Pinned to the wall is a photo of his grandfather who was clearly very dear to him. It shows an upright but old man, barefooted with a flattish woven straw hat and a soft expression.

Lama does not talk easily about himself but I know that he became a monk at the age of fifteen after his parents had separated. It was his grandfather who suggested he entered a monastery in order to continue to be looked after and gain an education. Children in difficulty continue to enter monasteries and nunneries in this way in Bhutan today. Lama is around eight years younger than me, although he can only guess at his birth date – something that is common in rural areas for a person in their forties or older as time was measured by the seasons of planting and harvesting.

He is shorter than me, stockily built and laughs a lot. He particularly laughs in the company of his friends and in groups. When he teaches me there is some laughter but usually it's pretty serious. Although younger than me in years he has already spent around thirty years in monastic training, including a long time in retreat, so he is absolutely my senior, as any teacher must be. Otherwise how can you place your feet in the imprints they have left behind?

I am sure some of his life and his monastic training must have been tough both in terms of living conditions and emotionally in living away from his family. I once asked him about this and he said it was 'hard'. As he said it his voice was totally relaxed. He was simply stating a fact. He was not emotionally tied to it. It was a big teaching. I used the word 'hard' a lot to describe the experience of bringing up Oscar but when I used it, it was not said with such freedom.

In asking Lama a little bit of his life and trying to piece his story together, I learnt that he took over looking after the temple at Dochula in late August 2011, a few weeks before my first visit to Bhutan. Prior to that time he would have been elsewhere in Bhutan or on retreat. If I had gone before that year I would not have met him. Despite wanting to go to Bhutan for so many years, in the end, the timing was just perfect.

CHAPTER 24

THE ROAD MAP

As far as I was concerned I had made it to a state of happily ever after. Things were easier all round. The anxious speed which had been running me for so long was finally fully dissolving, like a cloud being absorbed back into the sky.

I discovered I could let more things go. I was less outside, more inside – and that inside was much happier.

Lama was continuing to teach me and we had regular conversations on the phone, at least once a month. Our conversations were mostly geared towards asking a question that had arisen for me when doing my formal Buddhist prayer practice. Sometimes they were to do with the techniques of practice – how to pronounce something or how many times to repeat a line – but more often they were to help me reflect on how to apply what I was learning to my daily life. Lama acted like a mirror; his responses showing me my own thinking so I could better reflect on it. This is when I knew these practices were really helping me, at the school gate, in the supermarket queue. Everything was simpler, easier and far more stable.

So that was it. I had made a full recovery and surely I had now discovered what was meaningful in life. Surely I could sit back and relax – mentally at least – even though running round after Oscar didn't exactly allow me the life of a passive potato.

Ah, how wrong I was!

In November 2012, I was midway through one of our to-the-point telephone conversations when Lama said, 'Now it is time for you to change your dress.'

'What, Lama. Sorry?' was my reply.

'Now it is time for you to change your dress,' he repeated clearly.

Despite the oddly constructed phrase, I had an inkling of what he meant. *Is he telling me to become a nun?*

If so, it would be surprising for many reasons and unusual as he generally only gives me big instructions face-to-face.

'*Really*, Lama?' I wasn't sure what to say so I reverted to type and asked a question. 'How do you know this?'

He paused and then said, quietly, 'My inner voice has told me.'

So it had to be that. I wasn't going to argue with his inner voice which, up to this point, I had never heard mention of.

He was telling me to swap lay clothes (and I had a lot of them!) for a set of robes. Taken aback and overjoyed in equal measure, I shed a few tears and was rather incoherent in my amazement that he thought I could possibly become a nun.

'Thank you so much, Lama la,' I said and hung up in a state of shocked elation.

I thought about it properly and began to wonder. *What did he really mean?* Had Lama really just told me to become a nun? It had felt that way but I hadn't asked him this direct question.

I thought I'd better make quite sure. To get a second opinion I called Brent in Bhutan, who was by now a good friend and a wise sounding block having lived there for three years. He was particularly clear on Bhutanese customs and protocol and I was sure he would know what was going on.

'No, no,' said Brent firmly. 'He doesn't mean for you to become a nun. Just buy one of those apron things.'

Apron things? I was totally at a loss.

Worried that the translation between Dzongkha in Lama's head and English in Lama's mouth had gone awry, and definitely not wanting to do the wrong thing, I called Lama back.

'Lama, can I just check *exactly* what is it you want me to do now?'

'Go to the monk shop in Thimphu and buy the dress of an ani, OK?'

He seemed mildly annoyed at having to speak on this again. Lama does not waste words and, I guess, in his mind this issue had already been covered.

'Right. Got it.' I hurried to get off the phone now it had been made crystal clear.

I stayed sitting down for a while on my chair, downstairs in my little house in Whitstable.

So that was most definitely it. My Lama had instructed me to become a nun.

I sat quietly for a while, letting the feeling of happiness replace that of amazement. He had faith in me. I couldn't believe it.

It also means no sex… with anyone… ever again.

I thought about the cycle of relationships in my life, watching them as if they were floating downstream under a bridge. In particular I recalled lust, the feeling of lusting after someone physically. I knew what it felt like, that wanting. To be a contented nun, this kind of oomph and I would have to part company. Part of me knew it was a huge decision to commit to that life change but a bigger part of me felt perfectly ready for it and not worried at all.

Then I worked through the practicalities. I would need to buy robes and work out how to put them on. Neither of these would be very easy in England, where Buddhist clothing shops and nuns to explain what to buy aren't exactly thick on the ground. I would have to wait four weeks to my next visit to Bhutan and sort it then. I had been invited back to Bhutan to attend the first Bhutan Nuns Foundation conference which was to be held in the country, involving Buddhist nuns from a wide range of countries. I would have my new clothes just in time!

In Bhutan that December, I went straight to the monk shop in Thimpu which is near the little roundabout in the centre of the city, famous for its traffic officer in white gloves directing the traffic. This monk shop is one of two in the city and it has a Western-style mannequin by the doorstep, wearing an example of monk's clothing. The mannequin is about a foot taller than most Bhutanese, with a face you might see in the windows of Selfridges, but naturally it's a mannequin left without a wig. The one-roomed shop has three walls of open shelves, stacked with folded clothes in red, orange, yellow and saffron. Hanging from the ceiling on a pole are the thick, red monk jackets which are so useful in the winter months. I bought what I needed in there.

I asked the lady if I should have a spare set of the rounded cloth which would cover my lower body but she seemed taken aback by this idea. Why would I need two? I had been thinking of washing but of course one *is* sufficient. The main element of Himalayan Buddhist robes is this huge circle of material which is folded round the body and held in place by your elbows as you whip a woven 'belt' around the middle to keep the material in place. The belt has no fixings or buckle as Westerners might expect but is a simple band of densely woven fabric that's secured by tucking the ends back into itself. It took a bit of practice and various friends in Bhutan tended to tidy me up for a while but now I have it down pat.

This material and belt cover my lower body. Above them I wear a sleeveless top or a formal, red monastic top called a 'thong gak'. Across my whole body is a large piece of red-burgundy material, usually called a 'zen', which tucks under my right armpit and loops over my left shoulder. Both the nature of the top and the placement of the zen ensure your right arm is left bare, a symbol originating from the early years of Buddhism that you are peaceful and not concealing a weapon.

People have asked me if Lama's instruction to 'change my dress' put me into a dilemma. Did I mull over both sides, see advantages and disadvantages, write lists, go back and forth and back and forth? This often used to be my chosen method of decision-making in other areas of my life. But, no – *this* wasn't like that. I know it would be more dramatic if his suggestion had placed me in a state of high tension and confusion but it did not. It was all clear. If Lama thought I was capable of it then, yes, absolutely, I knew I wished to make this change.

It is a serious thing to move from being a layperson to being a monastic. It felt serious but not heavy; it was light as a cloud playing in the sky. A cloud back-bending and jumping and enjoying space, maybe even giggling; high on air.

Lama's kindness had inspired me. I had all the courage I needed to move. I knew this was the way to go.

My surprise was at being given this opportunity at all as I didn't think I fitted the known job description. Firstly, I had a child and surely that ruled me out. Secondly, I had a small grasp of Tibetan but not enough to even read the prayers properly. Thirdly, I had always doubted I had the discipline or concentration. Wasn't I commitment-phobic?

I had a conversation about this with Lama. I asked him to confirm that I could truly be a nun while raising a child. His response was: 'Yes, yes, fine. If you leave him you cause him suffering. Who else can fully look after him? Also, you have the mind of an ani.'

The mind of an ani?

'Ani' is the classical Tibetan word for 'nun'. I have heard different ideas as to its origin as a word. The one I like best is that the ཨ་(A)ནི(NI) means the 'perfection of emptiness'. Emptiness is a state of mind which realises the interdependence of all things. It's a big subject but it's worth saying that to realise this reality, this state of perfection, implies a highly developed mind, close to something like a Buddha's. 'Ani' could be a corruption of the Tibetan word for 'aunt' and implies, with a slightly sour taste, an unmarried woman. So this term can go high up into the lofty realms or it can stay low.

If I say the word 'ani' in the UK people tend to think of it as a woman's first name, as in *Annie Get Your Gun*. I like the word 'ani' and I prefer it to the clunky translation into the

English word 'nun', which is not a play on 'none', as in the Buddhist notion of emptiness.

I need to stress that the impact of wearing robes, not Western clothes, has been very liberating for me and I think a big part of why I feel more relaxed in my own skin. Despite doing fairly well on the attractiveness scales, my body and its marks out of ten was something I was frequently aware of. It took up a significant amount of my mental time and energy. Letting this go has brought me a deep sense of relaxation. Having no hair, no make-up and no more wiggle shoes has felt deeply freeing. This feeling of relaxation and happiness means I easily smile more. Perhaps in jeans and a top you would be a little wary of someone who keeps smiling but in robes it's fine. That's a definite upside.

For a short while it was a little strange going to Buddhist events in the West with a shaven head and robes while still calling myself 'Emma'. It's fine in everyday situations but in formal Buddhist settings it was rather odd. Usually monastics have a dharma name to inspire them, so 'Emma' needed to become something else. While I had had a name given to me at Samye Ling when I originally took refuge, now I was training in the Bhutanese tradition under a different teacher so it was best to have a new name given to me in Bhutan.

I should add here that the Bhutanese find my original name amusing. 'Ema' in Dzongkha means 'chilli' and is a key staple in their national dish of *ema datsi*, chilli and cheese with red rice. For a while I was the Chilli Nun.

I asked Lama for a Buddhist name, in line with the usual practice for an ani.

'Yes,' he said. 'It's right. We will ask Rinpoche.' (By 'we' he meant 'he'.)

'What, *the* rinpoche?'

'Yes. Rinpoche,' he said quietly.

'Oh. OK. Great.' I said, all the while thinking WOW inside but careful not to let it show in a tasteless fashion!

I had thought Lama would give me a name himself but he wanted to give me the best name he could, to help strengthen my ability to practise, so he was going up the ranks for me. A rinpoche is a Buddhist title given to a person who's recognised as a special meditation practitioner. To qualify they have to be able to recall facts from their previous life (or lives) as an accomplished Buddhist practitioner. In this way their definition differs from that of a lama.

I have been lucky enough to meet and listen to a few rinpoches, and it's increasingly possible to do this in the West. The rinpoche that Lama was referring to lives in Bhutan, usually residing high up in the hills over Thimphu at the main Buddhist university, Tango. Tango here means 'Head of the Horse', not a fizzy orange drink!

Lama took me to meet this rinpoche one summer. It was a profound meeting for me. Profound for me may sound like sci-fi to you but let's see.

I had tried to find some information on this rinpoche on the internet but had found nothing so I really had no idea what to expect.

We started early from Dochula and stopped in Thimphu to buy a plain round cake and fresh milk which we would be giving to the monks once we got there, as tradition dictated.

We continued the drive twenty minutes or so outside Thimpu until we reached the base of the monastery. We parked and Lama smiled over at a few local people as he got a large, brightly coloured umbrella out of his car boot. Lama's car was small and silver, of Indian origin. A recent addition to his life, it enables him to visit his home village to perform his duties there as well as other lama jobs.

The umbrella was very useful on the way up. Although it didn't rain, the winding path was steep and I used it to dig into the muddy path, leaning my body weight on it to lever me up the criss-crossing mountain path. Along the way a series of small signs, written in gold on red backgrounds and placed in brown wooden frames, had been attached to the trees at eye height. They created a good reason/excuse to pause and catch your breath.

If you want to know your past
Look at who you are today.
If you want to know your future
Look at your mind today.

These words were pinned to a silvery tree. I read it twice, the second time slowly and out loud into my collar to help me remember it.

After another twenty minutes of walking we reached a large prayer wheel and sat to the side of it, opposite each other, on the handily positioned wooden benches.

During this time of rest the sounds of birds gradually got louder than my own breathing and Lama began to explain the correct protocol when meeting a rinpoche. We would do three prostrations (moving your body from upright to bowing down, head and hands to the floor and up again) on entering the room and then we might be asked to sit down. I needed to know in advance that sitting down would not necessarily be the case. It seemed a big walk to not sit down and chat at the end but, OK, Lama had sensibly lowered my expectations so there was no way I could be disappointed.

Arriving at the monastery was a relief after the steep climb. Lama was greeted with great respect from monks close to the entrance gate. He had studied and then become a teacher at Tango before being appointed to the temple at Dochula. The monks showed their respect through the custom of putting their hand in front of their mouth when speaking to him. I waited a little behind him, watching and feeling my breath settle down to something closer to a resting pace. He turned round to check where I was and then walked forwards, through the gate and into the main part of the monastery.

I tagged along, smiling whenever possible and trying not to forget what I was seeing. Whitewashed walls with golden prayer wheels set into them formed an outside corridor to walk beside on the route to entering the main building. At the end of this wall we entered and went straight into a large room filled with long tables covered with shiny plastic tablecloths and simple benches to sit on – the main dining hall. We joined the monks for Bhutanese-style tea out of plastic mugs and cream crackers stacked up in a large bowl. In Bhutan tea can be butter tea, sweet tea or milk tea. There were monks but also laypeople moving around. They were probably visiting the monastery as a pilgrimage or to see relatives living there as monks. We sat down with three other monks and Lama talked away in Dzongkha, happy to see old friends. I stayed silent and drank my milky tea, looking at the pictures of great past teachers on the walls. Given my height I thought perhaps I might be mistaken for a monk if I stayed quiet and it might be easier to blend in.

On finishing, Lama got up and, looking down at me, smiled and said in English, 'Time to go.'

We walked to the inner courtyard of the monastery, towards the rinpoche's quarters. Things got quieter once we were in the anteroom, waiting. There was a lot of wood and whispering. We handed the cake and milk to an attendant standing near us. I waited quietly and noticed Lama becoming serious and rather solemn in a way I had not seen before. Then Lama made a slight gesture with his hand to encourage me to move forward. I followed him dipped my head to pass under the small wooden door and into the room.

Once inside, standing side by side, we did our three prostrations. It was not easy to do these prostrations; I was holding the white offering scarf folded up in my left hand and, at the same time, I was unwrapping and rewrapping the red zen material around my body. As you prostrate and bow down you open this material, touch the floor with your head and hands then rewrap it across you when you stand back up. I fumbled, trying to keep up with the ease and speed with which Lama performed his prostrations. I did not want to fall over my feet and land on my nose as I had in PE lessons years back with Miss Dingle.

Then I kept my head down and moved towards a seated figure somewhere over there. As I did so I felt the wooden planks of the floor rising and falling under my feet as if I was walking on rolling thunder.

What on earth is going on?

My whole body started to shake uncontrollably, like the turbulence in a plane about to cause the luggage to fall out. I was not able to lift my head to look up.

Lama continued forwards and I followed. It looked like we were in fact going to be sitting down. Still looking down, I sat. Lama began talking quietly in Dzongkha to the rinpoche and I became stiller as the shaking left my body. As Lama talked, I was able to look up and see a young man sitting in bright yellow and red robes with round glasses. There he was, something extraordinary in a human body. I would have sat beside him for ever. When someone is that magnetic you have to reign in your groupie tendencies. I guess John Lennon found the same, wearing similar glasses.

Struck dumb, dumbstruck, I managed to ask him a question about the nature of anger which was still a subject I was keen to understand to help with daily life.

His answer involved emptiness. There it was again.

Emptiness.

After the meeting all I could say to Lama was, 'Wow.'

He knew what I meant. Some things don't need whole sentences. Imagine a perfect sphere of light which is constantly exploding, sending light outwards into a limitless space. Perhaps this rinpoche proved the physics of bliss. Perhaps if he lay down on his right side he would simply become a reclining Buddha.

This was the rinpoche that Lama wanted to give me a monastic name.

I waited back in England and, sure enough, a few days later, Lama sent me a text (this was possible now as Bhutan was fast moving to a mobile world): *Rinpoche has named you Pema Deki. It means Blissful Lotus.*

I called him for more details.

Lama had a fit of the giggles.

'Ha, ha. He named you Pema when you were Emma. Emma Pema.'

Lama found it particularly funny as the rinpoche had not known my English name. We both agreed my mum had nearly got it right. It was a short conversation for a re-birth.

Emma to Pema. The Chilli to the Lotus. It had been quite a journey.

CHAPTER 25

DIRECTIONS

As I write this I realise my decisions may sound odd to you. Here I was having shaved my head, put on robes and adopted a monastic name yet I was still shopping in Tesco and putting screen wash in my little car. But it felt so right and all the changes I had made were making my life feel complete.

I was loving being a nun. I felt fully alive in a way I never had before. It was an unusual opportunity and only possible due to the flexible thinking of my Bhutanese Lama. There are examples within the Himalayan tradition of practitioners having children and then putting on robes but they are more often men than women from what I have seen and usually the child might be older when the parent took on full robes. It is a big job raising a child and following the dedicated practice required of a Buddhist nun. The notion of parenthood as a valid part of a spiritual path remains one for debate and I struggle to find similar role models to look to.

Perhaps I am too Western and too modern but I feel there are real insights and benefits which come from experiencing both lay and monastic life. It has been a real challenge to combine these two roles. As any parent will tell you, the qualities of patience and kindness are essential. For me the easier path would have been to leave Oscar and join a monastery or go into retreat. Perhaps it would have been more 'proper' but as Lama had made clear it would also cause Oscar great suffering. I am his mum and I love him hugely and at this stage in his life my presence and love and support are crucial.

At times I have felt slightly embarrassed at the apparent double life I lead. I have no doubt that doing one *or* the other would have been easier and, perhaps, more acceptable. In some Buddhist societies the continued presence of Oscar in my life could be seen as a negative, a distraction from pure concentration on Buddhist studies, but these were not considerations which entered my head when Lama suggested it.

If I didn't appreciate how much becoming a nun has enabled me to fully come alive and be a far kinder person, doubts and questions over my precise definition might have weighed me down. But out of this awareness of my own mind settling, many things began to arise.

Firstly there grew a determination to practise and gain greater understanding. Secondly grew the wish to help others, initially in my mind and, then, in action.

Formal daily practice requires determination. It's like a job, except you're not paid for it and only you know if you have actually done it or not. So it also requires total honesty – only you know if your mind is really changing. People I chat to are often surprised when they realise I'm dedicating so much of my time to doing formal practices for 'nothing'. I guess it could appear to be self-indulgent or escapist therapy but it's not. For me, the bottom line is: it works.

For all the hours of formal practice (prayers and meditations) my mind is not being pulled back and forth to the ego and the question of what *I* want and what *I* don't want. Going from this *to* that, this *or* that; this mental habit which is so tiring for the human mind. Days, weeks and years of formal practice is a lot of time *being* in a different way. This alone is very powerful for rewiring the neural networks of the brain and establishing new, more positive and wiser paths of thinking.

When I am in England I practise in my little house. When I am in Bhutan I like to spend some time practising at a little lhakang in Paro that Brent told me about. Aware that I had been practising compassion for a long time, he mentioned that I should visit Dungtse Lhakang. It was built by a famous Tibetan master, probably in the fifteenth century. The lhakang is unusual in that it's round in shape and made up of three layers, like a wedding cake, each layer reached internally by an old wooden ladder. Inside it is extremely dark so it's best to use a torch or a candle. If you are not practised at climbing a ladder with a couple of loose rungs, in the dark, holding a candle at the same time, it's best to decide on a torch. I have seen Paro women climb the ladder, candle in hand, young child strapped to their back with a striped piece of material.

These days I remain downstairs when I visit this lhakang. I sit on the ground floor, in front of a beautiful 7-ft-high painting of the representation of compassion Chenrezig, who is painted with 1,000 arms surrounding him to signify his wish to help beings without limit. In winter sitting on the lhakang's floor is cold as some concrete has been added

– wise given the darkness and the need for candles – and I have been known to take a duvet in with me. In summer it is beautifully cool and restful.

I like having built a connection to one main sacred place to sit down in, in Bhutan. It means I recognise the people circumambulating the lhakang enough to say hello. If it's cold, and I'm sitting inside for long periods, the caretaker family bring me milk tea in a melamine cup with little flowers on it, and cream crackers with sugar crystals stuck on top of them to keep me going. In the spring the orange tree outside attracts beautiful, tiny songbirds and this gives the tree the appearance of shrilly calling to the sky.

These places of local culture and faith are very restful. I am very grateful for them. They have allowed me to relax into formal practice, reducing the sense that meditation practice is somehow a separate thing from the daily habits of life. I may be a tall, white woman dressed in the red nun's robes of the Himalayas but inside this lhakang, doing practice, I feel profoundly at home.

Formal practices can include the compassion practices, such as the repetition of the *Om mani peme hung* mantra Karin and I were doing on our first visit to Bhutan. They can also include something called 'ngondro', which means 'preliminary practice'. This was the practice I had briefly considered doing years ago following the break-up with Peter.

This ngondro practice leads on to the study of 'Mahamudra' (a Sanskrit term meaning 'Great Gesture'; 'Chagya Chenpo' is the phonetic Tibetan). The Mahamudra teachings are ones I may, one day, get from my Lama. I presume they are advanced practices for the training of the mind but, as I have not learnt them yet, I cannot describe them from my own experience. The ngondro forms the path towards these teachings.

After a few more months of continued compassion practice and teachings, Lama asked if I was interested in doing this ngondro. I knew it was a significant, time-consuming practice and that it was considered essential for a monastic so I agreed.

Having suggested the idea, Lama then followed up with, 'Oh, but it's very hard to do. Very difficult for you, I think.' He laughed. 'Even Bhutanese find it hard and you, *you* are a Westerner.'

Perhaps he knows this is a sure way to get me motivated.

'No, no, I would like to do this, Lama. Please teach me,' I said firmly.

'OK, OK. I get book for you.'

'Is there a book with the English translation, do you think?' I was thinking through the practicalities.

'Maybe, maybe. Yes, I think I have seen it one time.'

We had a plan.

Still I would have to make sure to follow it. It had only taken a few words but I had already committed to completing a big practice. I knew it would add so much to my understanding and capacity to be free from harmful mental habits of anger and desire. I was also aware it would be a huge daily time commitment and would mean I would have to be very disciplined if I was to manage it all while being a mum to Oscar, managing all the usual things of life. It also meant I would have to keep returning to Bhutan for teachings which was great but would also require a financial commitment. I knew all of this and had no doubt I wished to do it all.

On my next visit four months later, he gave me the book, the ngondro text written in Tibetan with a line-by-line English translation underneath. I thought he might begin to teach me it at that point but he just told me to read it and become familiar with some key phrases. I was keen to start but there's no pushing a mountain in the shape of a lama.

I returned to England and continued to read this text and form some questions to discuss with him. On my next visit to Bhutan, Lama sang the text to me at great speed. This oral giving of a text is an essential part of the way Vajrayana Buddhist practices are passed from teacher to student. It can be considered a form of blessing. After that I thought we would start the instruction itself. But no. We discussed my questions and left it at that, with Lama repeating, 'It's very difficult. I think you find it very difficult.'

I made plans to return again, impressing on Lama that I really *was* wishing to be taught the ngondro now. Bear in mind that it was costing money flipping back and forth to Bhutan with an orange book waiting to be given the green light to start. I was not sure how sustainable my Bank Loan For Bhutan was.

In November 2013 I returned yet again as Oscar was with Mark for a few days; both of us going was a much bigger financial outlay and I was increasingly coordinating Mark's holiday days with Oscar with trips to Bhutan.

Brent offered to lend me a room in his house close to the hotel where Lama could begin to give me the first teachings of ngondro. Aum Sonam brought in butter lamps and incense and prepared a small shrine for us. Beginning a new practice such as this needs all the help it can get and all these elements are considered essential. Aum Sonam had, by this time, become a real friend. Perhaps a little wary at first at my apparent enthusiasm to study Buddhism, she was beginning to see this was no passing fad.

Lama arrived and got out of his little silver car.

After the usual greetings I was quick to cut to the chase.

'It's wonderful to see you, Lama. I am so happy to be getting my ngondro instructions at last.'

'Ah yes,' he said. 'No, I think today we will just discuss.'

I could have bonked myself on the forehead.

'No, Lama. No. *Please* give me the teachings.' I was totally clear. Enough; I was ready.

He laughed easily and happily. 'OK, OK, you are right, let's go.'

He walked ahead, after Brent and Aum Sonam, towards the house where it had all been prepared for us. The path was dusty and dog-strewn the minute we passed through the back gate of the hotel and on to Brent's house. I followed after him, quite happy to be a poodle. I was about to start ngondro.

These teachings are not most people's idea of winning the lottery. They involve an enormous amount of hard work. It's not like getting a day out at a spa. As with the compassion practices, which are designed to deliberately develop compassion in the mind, the ngondro is a set of practices designed to train the mind to deliberately turn away from habits of ego-attachment, anger and pride. In clearing these mental clouds they then allow the mind to open, into habits of kindness towards others and the development of generosity, patience and concentration. Buddhists talk of 'mind poisons' which begin with an attachment to self and which can be seen as having similarity to the seven deadly sins spoken of in other traditions. The practices of ngondro help the practitioner clear themselves of these mind poisons.

These ngondro practices are also seen as essential to getting a person ready for the later meditation trainings. It's like preparing the ground of your mind for the planting of a precious plant. First making the ground level, then removing any stones and ensuring it's free draining.

These preliminary practices are very intense and time consuming. They are divided into four sets of 110,000 repetitions which come to a total of 440,000.

The first of the four practices is prostrations (as we had done three times to the rinpoche at Tango), which are performed 110,000 times along with visualisations, prayers and reflections. This was to take me nine months, averaging six hours' practice every day. In a basic way you could connect this practice to sun salutations in Hatha yoga (the yoga of body and breath).

Sometimes I got up at 4 a.m. to begin them while Oscar was asleep, sometimes I did them while he was at school or with Mark. It was a daily commitment which I continued to make but I had to be flexible on precisely when it happened.

It was not easy. Towards the end, with large and tired arm muscles, I can remember calling Lama and describing myself as an ant walking up Mount Everest! But I completed it to time with my next visit to Bhutan. I knew Lama would not give me the next instructions over the phone so I made sure to complete them before seeing him. I thought we might have a big chat about it all and its meaning – but not really. The only question Lama asked me about completing the practice was: 'Do you appreciate you?'

This was confusing to me. *What did he mean?* I wondered? *Do I appreciate me?*

I thought it might be a trick question to see if I still had pride or ego.

'Eh, I don't really know, Lama.'

'You must appreciate *you*. It's not easy to do this.'

'Right, OK, Lama.'

I gained my next instructions to begin the full practice of the 100-syllable mantra which is repeated 110,000 times along with visualisations, prayers and reflections. The benefits of repeating this long mantra are very much connected to the deeper koshas, particularly through the vibrational effects of sound on the whole person. In some ways, you could connect this practice to a form of bhakti yoga (yoga of devotion) or jnana yoga (yoga of scriptural study). Lama had asked me to learn this mantra a while back on my way to teach the nuns at Bumthang so I had a head start on this one. Again completing the 110,000 took about nine months.

The third practice is making a mandala offering, which includes placing wheat or rice in specific positions on a piece of metal called a mandala plate before washing them away with saffron water. Again this is done 110,000 times along with prayers, visualisations and reflections. This practice could be seen as connected to karma yoga (yoga of selfless action) and bhakti yoga (devotional yoga). This one was tough; you have to hold a metal mandala plate in front of you for hours as you make the mandalas. It was a very helpful practice in terms of letting go of selfishness but my left shoulder muscles were very happy when I finished it.

The final practice is guru yoga, which also uses mantras, visualisations, prayers and reflections and is repeated 110,000 times. This practice is designed to connect to subtler parts of consciousness and could be seen as connected to raja yoga (yoga of the mind) and bhakti yoga (yoga of devotion). This practice went faster than the rest but I will continue to study it further, particularly as the Tibetan is long and I need to work on my pronunciation.

There are different ways to perform these practices but the way I am taught is very simple. I must do some of the particular practice I am on every day until I have completed that set of 110,000. Only then do I move on to the next set of 110,000 repetitions. If a day is missed I would have to return to the start of that set and write off any of the repetitions so far accumulated – that's a great incentive to keep doing them every day! You keep track of the repetitions by counting your mala beads and noting down totals in a book – not that you tend to forget the number you are on!

The number of repetitions is useful in retraining the neural pathways of the brain, as neuroscience is helping to show us. It would be easy to go through the motions of these repetitions but done with integrity they are ways in which to see your own mind, your own motivations change for the better. I find them very, very helpful.

Ngondro is a practice often done in retreat, when it is completed in a number of months. Practised outside retreat circumstances, as I have done it, woven into daily life, it takes significantly longer. It took me just over three years to complete the 440,000 practices, finishing them in 2016. It was a bit like digging a pit, going down, deeper and deeper through the levels of the mind. Who knows what will be at the bottom? Who knows what you will be able to see when you look up? I know from experience that what is growing underneath is not always obvious from the surface.

CHAPTER 26

ORDINATION

At the end of 2013 I had been wearing robes for a year and had had a shaven head for longer than that. By then people were expecting me to look that way. I was halfway through the ngondro and beginning to feel the benefits of training the mind away from the negative.

My family had embraced my decision, seeing how happy it was clearly making me. Oscar said he was proud of me and continued to say that I looked the happiest mum at the school pickup. He had been showing his class where Bhutan was on a map and pointing out that lamas weren't only four-legged creatures that spat at you.

At first Whitstable had craned a little at the neck on seeing me walk past. My friend Richard said it was always useful to take me on a walk as cars always stopped for us at zebra crossings! After a good year though, no one gave me a second glance; my red robes had become part of the Whitstable scenery. It was a good feeling.

I had got to know people from teaching yoga, then through Oscar who had changed schools to a smaller one to help him cope better. Lots of people said hello because I looked friendly or different or both. For the first time I was realising that no matter where I was, I had the feeling of being at home, of fitting in. All the time. I didn't only feel happy in Bhutan. I was relieved at that because otherwise life could have got difficult in Whitstable.

I was aware that, although I was following vows, I had not yet had a formal ceremony to confirm the use of the word 'ani'. I asked Lama if I should formalise my vows in some way. I was not sure how this happened or what the rules were. There was certainly no manual for this in Bhutan and looking it up on the internet did not help.

Lama said he would ask Dorji Lopen, the number two in terms of the monastic structure of Bhutan, if he would let me take the necessary vows. I was only vaguely aware of who Dorji Lopen was – again, there's no use looking for him on Wikipedia. I was to discover later that he had done nine years in retreat and is a totally awesome individual.

I left Bhutan in January 2014 and waited for Lama to tell me if the Lopen had agreed.

He didn't call so after a month I phoned him to ask.

As if it were of little matter, Lama said that Dorji Lopen had agreed to do it.

'Great,' I said. 'When?'

'Oh, I don't know about that.'

Hmm. No clear plan? I really should be getting used to this by now. Maybe it was tricky for Lama to pin down Dorji Lopen to a particular time; like trying to organise your boss.

I decided to borrow some money again and return to Bhutan for a week with Oscar in February 2014 and chance it. February is an auspicious month in the Buddhist calendar with Losar, the Buddhist New Year, falling at that time.

We arrived in Bhutan after the multistage journey and six-hour time difference. It was lovely to see Brent, his dogs, Aum Sonam and other friends back in Paro.

Once at the hotel, Oscar crashed out and went to bed. I called Lama to say we were in Bhutan and ask if he thought the ceremony might happen on this visit.

'I don't know. I will call,' came his answer.

I waited for a while then went to bed too.

At ten that night the phone rang in the dark. I grabbed at it on my side table, keen not to wake Oscar. He was snoring like a good 'un though, as he does when he is really tired.

It was Lama. 'We go tomorrow. It will happen Wednesday.'

'Oh, that's great, Lama. Thank you.'

I hadn't expected it to happen quite so soon – it was ten o'clock at night on Monday. In my head it felt like another time in some other country.

'Shall we meet at Dochula tomorrow then, Lama?'

'Yes, come there. I will see you then.'

'OK. Bye, Lama.'

Still dazed, I blearily got back on the phone to begin organising a car, a driver, accommodation in Punakha and a 9 a.m. start. All the while, Oscar's snores kept me down to earth.

I got up in the dark room and called Mum in England from my mobile. 'Mum, it's happening. It will be on Wednesday at around 4 a.m. in the morning UK time.'

She was thrilled. 'That's wonderful news, Emma. I am so happy for you. Many congratulations.' It was great to hear her support.

'Thanks, Mum. I really can't believe it.'

I would have called more people but I needed to get some sleep and so lay down in the large bed with a big smile on my face, looking into the darkness.

Waking in the morning, I shared my excitement with Oscar.

'Osc, guess what happened while you were asleep? Lama called,' I said, asking and answering my own question at the same time.

'Great,' said Oscar. 'Did you get your upgrade?'

'Yes,' I laughed. 'Lama said Mummy is getting her upgrade. So now we have to get up, young man. We'll get our breakfast and go.'

We got a car and a new driver as Tshering was in East Bhutan and we drove to Dochula. Lama was standing waiting for us by the 108 chortens as we drove up, the Himalayas blue and white in front of us. We got out and into his little silver car for the rest of the journey to Punakha. When I first met Lama he did not have a car but he got one so he can travel to his home village and to various religious commitments around the country. He was a very slow driver to begin with but now he is very competent, keeping a spare set of robes and white scarves in the back for any occasion.

Oscar was excited to be sitting in the front as Lama drove. I joined in with the conversation from the back. Lama sought out a Western music station on the car radio. Elton John began singing 'Candle in the Wind'. *Goodbye Norma Jean*.

'Oh, Lama, you must know this.'

He smiled. 'No.'

I thought about Marilyn Monroe, that skirt, the hair, JFK. I tried a different tack.

'Lama la, you do know who Elvis Presley is, right?'

He laughed. 'No, no. Why?'

I hadn't thought there was a person on earth who had not heard of Elvis Presley.

It is common in Bhutan to add 'la' after people's names when addressing them directly. It's a term of respect and I try to remember to add a 'la' to everyone I meet.

Punakha, the ancient capital of Bhutan, is about an hour and a half's drive from Dochula. We had to drive from the high, cold altitude of Dochula down through increasingly bright green, layered hills, tiered to allow the most efficient form of rice cultivation. We dropped a total of 1,850m down to 1,200m above sea level. Oscar's ears were deaf for a while as they adjusted. He thought it was hilarious, giving him a chance to get away with some seriously theatrical shouting.

On the journey, I asked Lama whom he had taken his getsul vows with.

'With Dorji Lopen,' he said.

Even sitting in the back of the car, I could tell he was smiling from the way his ears moved.

'Oh, Lama, I did not realise.'

This meant a great deal to me. I would be taking my getsulma vows with the same person he had taken such vows with. The vows would be continuing from his teacher, to him and down to me. We were becoming something like a family.

'Getsul' vows are the novice vows and are the most common form of vows held by women practising in the Himalayan tradition. The vows are usually called 'getsulma' vows for women, the 'ma' added to specify a female.

I stayed quiet in the back, digesting it all and letting the bright green fields and mottled sky wash over me until we arrived in Punakha.

This ancient capital is a powerful place. It has one of the largest Bhutanese dzongs and is located at the meeting point of two rivers. One of these rivers is described as being female in nature, one described as being male. When these two rivers meet it is considered helpful to build a place of power and spiritual practice. I thought at first it meant it was an auspicious place and so the building of a dzong there was some kind of celebration, but no, it's because it's not an auspicious place and so it needs the good fortune a dzong can bring.

Lama drove us to a small hotel by a river of uncertain gender and then he went off to the dzong to make arrangements for the next day. Oscar and I walked to the stony side of the river and built round circles out of the stones on the wide, dry bank.

After a while Oscar decided to create a detective story about a murder which had happened there and started to look for clues, giving me a running commentary on the gory story. As he talked, I rested my gaze on the birds landing on grey stones lining the river's edge. They were orange-coloured ducks with plump tummies, landing and taking off with ease.

As I relaxed, watching the sun catch the water and the shiny backs of the ducks, my mind wandered back. I remembered another Emma walking quickly in suit and heels, company reports tucked under her arm, leaving the Hong Kong office for a presentation lunch. I could see her speed, her face driven by the wish to understand. If I had called out to her then, she would not have heard. If I had tried to sit her down and show her the future, she would have pushed me aside in her haste to follow her schedule. I felt a kind of sorrow for her, seeing her efforts and her tension because I knew she had not been happy. I found myself caring for her. I felt so pleased that she had been given the chance to escape from that life. Thank you, Jakarta. Thank you, Michael. If this *was* karma then so be it. I felt a quiet prayer for all the years that had gone before being here, by this river in Bhutan, and, gazing across fields, I vaguely wondered where things would go from here.

Later that afternoon Lama returned to our hotel to have tea and confirm that it was all arranged for tomorrow at 9.30 a.m. He would pick us up at 9 a.m.

'Great,' I said. 'Now, Lama la, how can I prepare? Can you give me something to read and practise? You know my Tibetan is not good yet.'

'Ah, yes, and Dorji Lopen does tend to mumble,' said Lama.

My nerves began to kick in while I took in my surprise that Lama knew words like mumble.

'But no.' Lama said he was not able to give me anything to read or practise.

I would be going in cold.

The next morning Oscar took his model of the Tower of London (I had brought him something suitable for filling in time – a 'cut out and slot together' cardboard model of this London landmark). With Lama we drove to the dzong, the huge, white and windowed building at the meeting point of the two rivers. Bright prayer flags on high posts mingling with a scattering of trees loosely marked out the domain of the dzong. Lama was carrying my new saffron-patched zen, an offering bowl with money, rice, a white offering scarf and a red square of material for me to sit on. It was all in a bag by his side. He determinedly stepped onwards, Oscar and I following after his forward-set shoulders. It was a bright late winter day and still early so there were not many people about.

We went up the wide, steep wooden steps of the dzong and past two large prayer wheels inside the entrance. We walked to the left, then forwards, passing the tree which grows in the central courtyard. As we did so the large black crows nesting high up in the crannies of the central temple flew up. They scattered, circling in the sky, calling out their singular sound, taking over the space. I couldn't resist a smile at the memory of sitting on a warm balcony in Greece.

Next we all walked over and up some external wooden stairs to the Lopen's residence on the first floor. We settled Oscar and his Tower of London in a waiting room with two monks. Lama and I walked the few steps down a corridor to meet the Dorji Lopen. The feeling was one of quiet intensity. These were serious steps to be taking. This was the walk towards confirming I would live under vows for the rest of my life.

Once in the room, Lama remained standing. I sat cross-legged on the red square of material Lama had brought with him, in front of Dorji Lopen. He was already seated behind a small prayer table with various objects on it and a thick text in its usual paper covering (not a bound Western book but an unbound series of horizontal pages about 10 inches by 2 inches which is typical for any Buddhist text). I noticed his high-ranking robes, his soft face and gently dimpled upper arm, natural for a man in later life. I wondered if he had gone into retreat in a cave or a retreat house.

Sitting in front of him with Lama to my left, Dorji Lopen started, in Dzongkha, by impressing on me that he had not given these vows to a woman before and that I should be aware of this. Lama translated.

Do you remember that *Tom and Jerry* cartoon where Tom swallows a sofa and his eyes bulge, knowing he can't digest it all in one go?

Gulp.

I concentrated as hard as I could. Dorji Lopen quickly realised he had to speak the Tibetan sentences in small, bite-sized pieces if I was to successfully repeat them back to him as is required in the taking of vows.

I watched as he turned over the horizontal pages of text, placing them on the front pile so there were now two clear piles, read and unread. Gradually the back pile got smaller and the front one got bigger. Using this text Dorji Lopen spoke and, at certain points, I had to repeat his words back to him, mostly to confirm the taking of various vows. After each one he was to click his fingers to seal the vow in place.

As the ceremony continued I could feel the warmth of the sun coming in through the ornate, wooden windows close to the right side of my face. Below us was the sunlit river which ran by the dzong. My knees slightly sore from kneeling and my armpits sweaty from the concentration required to not mispronounce *too* much of the Tibetan. I have never been married but I am sure it must be a similar feeling where the people involved wish more than anything in the world to be there and to make those vows. At various points I did prostrations and prayers with Dorji Lopen as Lama stood to one side. Towards the end my name was once again confirmed as Pema Deki and then we were all smiling. It was done.

We walked back down the corridor to get Oscar and drove to park near the riverside. It must have been the male river as it was running fast, breaking over rocks. It was hot, nearly midday, and the sun shone off the water as it moved.

Oscar 'taught' Lama to build circles of stones; three outer rings with an upstanding stone in the centre. Lama found a twig to add to it, sticking up in the middle; making it a construction somewhere between a castle and a mandala. I was still grinning in a rather useless fashion.

An orange dinghy of river-rafting tourists passed by, taking photos of a Bhutanese lama, a Western ani and a child building distinct shapes on the river's stony edge. The cameras went off, the visitors standing up in the floating boat. Perhaps they thought this was a strange Buddhist custom being observed in this Himalayan kingdom.

After the ceremony and for the next couple of days I felt incredibly strong, invincible. The ceremony and formal confirmation of following vows definitely added clarity to what I was doing. I will be forever grateful to my Lama that he guided me to this formal ceremony of connection. It must have taken courage on his part to make this request.

What was so important about doing this? What did it change? This ceremony made me as small as a shining grain of sand and as huge as the open sea. The happiness of it was beyond any letters I can put together.

I can remember the feeling, as a child, of having found all the edge jigsaw pieces and joined them up. The next step was to collect all the internal pieces and work out what fitted with what. I always left the inside of the sky to the end as it was the trickiest part. I would savour placing the final piece in, creating the moment when many pieces become a seamless whole. The glossy surface of the puzzle would catch the light and shine up at me. Perfect.

THE POLLEN FROM
THE FLOWER

Walk with me right up to the top.

Come, stand by me.

Here above the treeline

Where the air is clear.

Shape your mouth and blow at clouds.

Ready?

Come on, let's jump from mountaintop

to mountaintop and sing a song of joy.

CHAPTER 27

MOTHERHOOD –
CLOSE BY AND FAR AWAY

I had thought that what I'd been working towards was simplification and in some ways this was what had happened. I now had my robes; all my other clothes and shoes had been given away. I had given up a lot of the hobbies or extracurricular activities of a layperson, which meant I had more time for the life I had chosen.

I was doing my best to remember ahimsa, the practice of non-violence or compassion to all beings. It was not always possible, especially if I became very tired in the course of the day. But I was trying every day – no matter what the previous day had held – to get up and remember this profound wish to develop kindness. This was ultimately why I had become a Buddhist.

But in other ways, rather than things getting simpler they seemed to be gaining momentum reminiscent of the way Oscar whizzes down the 'wall of death' slide at the play park. The more adept he gets the faster he goes; the more courage he gains the more adept he gets…

In February 2015, a year after being ordained, I travelled to an isolated part of South West Bhutan and a small village called Meritsemo. I was there at the request of the local lama who had asked me to visit his monastery and meet his small group of young monks. He had said they were really struggling to survive. He hoped I might be able to help them in some way.

In the years I've been visiting Bhutan I have helped people on a personal, informal basis. It's been my pleasure to. I had briefly met this lama in Thimphu on a previous visit but had explained that I was very busy and did not have time to do a lot to help. I explained that I might be able to offer £400–500 by running a yoga day in England on their behalf but that I did not feel I could do more than that. I said to him, with a knowing smile, 'I'm not Bill Gates, you know!' He stared back at me, clueless, as my reference fell flat.

Having decided I could not do much to help, I did agree to see the monastery's circumstances for myself that February. The travel company allocated me a driver, Norbu; a guide, Rinzin; and a four-by-four. Rinzin was very tall for a Bhutanese and seemed very polite and well-mannered. He was helpful and intensely private all at the same time, as many Bhutanese are. Norbu was a more mischievous chap who claimed to understand little English but grinned frequently at my jokes with Rinzin as I tried to win his confidence and bring him out of his shell.

We spent a mellow two days together before the trip south to Meritsemo. I took time to do some prayers at Dungtshe Lhakang. Norbu played on his Galaxy Samsung waiting in the car and Rinzin rested on the side of it, greeting Paro friends as they passed by walking down the hill into town. Forty-eight hours later, having adjusted to the time difference and altitude, we began the six-hour journey south from Paro to the village of Méritsemo. This would be the most rural and remote part of Bhutan I had seen to date. It had been tricky to work out accommodation on our trip so we had arranged to stay a night at a local college which had rooms in Gedu. It was chilly. Rinzin wore his knitted hat, Norbu wore everything he had and I felt far too hairless as we laughed over our rice dinner in the college staff canteen. Our breath was little white clouds blowing at each other so cold was the evening by then. After that I think we settled into each other more easily and Norbu began to slowly add in the occasional sentence to our conversations. I loved hearing him talk as he had such a beautiful up-down lilt to his voice which sounded as if it had never spoken a moment of anger or anxiety. It reminded me of the sing-song rhythm of a child's nursery rhyme, gently sung to lull you into sleep.

The next morning we left the college campus and started along the bumpy road to the village. Small stone posts along the route helpfully counted down the way and, an hour and a half later, we were approaching a small hill in the midst of a larger green valley. Coming from it were the haunting notes of monastic instruments as if the hill itself was calling out for help.

As we drove up the little hill to park by the small lhakang we saw the young monks and their instruments lined up, intent on doing their best. I am the mother of a young boy as well as a nun and such scenes raise different emotions in me. I wanted to speak to the young monks individually in order to understand more about what I was seeing and clarify my thoughts. As can often be the case in poor rural areas these monks had joined the monastery partially to study Buddhism but also because their families did not have the means to properly care for them or educate them. This Meritsemo lama quietly explained how a couple had come from broken homes where the new parenting arrangements did not welcome these children. It was sad but this time I was able to respond to this sadness differently. I could feel it touch something in me and it was something strong; a determination to help..

I returned from Meritsemo to England, mentally focused on doing what I could to help. And I mean *really* focused. The years of dedicated and disciplined ngondro practice had made me much more capable of focusing.

I set up a fundraising initiative with the help of many of my yoga students. One of my yoga students, Adrienne, a mother of two young girls, was keen to help. I was so grateful for her support. My background in finance and analysis complemented her artistic and photographic background. We were a good combination and, together, we set about making plans. We named the fundraising scheme Opening Your Heart to Bhutan and managed to persuade Simon, an IT friend, to help us set up a website and print flyers for free. We concentrated on raising money to renovate the young monks' sleeping quarters and build them a cold shower, two toilets, and the necessary connecting septic tank.

It was a success. We raised enough to bring these basic facilities to the young monks in a few short months. Rinzin oversaw the work and everything went amazingly smoothly.

It was hard to believe I could be in Whitstable overseeing the building of a septic tank in Bhutan – but it happened.

It began to dawn on me that a deeper commitment to Bhutan might be beginning and one that would require me to have enough funds to keep paying for flights and accommodation on more altruistic trips to the Himalayas. Although I might not occasionally need to pay the full tourist rate if I had a formal invitation to visit, I knew funds would always be required. It was still something to be aware of – but not something to hold me back.

Adrienne and I discussed the potential future aims of fundraising, particularly in light of further research I had done on poverty in Bhutan. We decided to expand our work into projects which would help the whole village: the young monks, the village primary school and the poorest families. While the monks' situation was tough, it was not much better for certain families in the village, so it seemed wisest to go forward on an entire village basis so all the children could benefit. This would also ensure no bad feeling in terms of the relationship between the monks and the lay villagers.

I needed to organise a second visit to the village. So at the end of May 2015, having raised more funds for the village, I borrowed money from my mum (mildly embarrassing at the age of 48!) and, with Oscar, travelled back to Bhutan. It was his school half-term and I had to take the opportunity to return. I needed to check the completed building works and I was eager to discuss the wider needs of the village and village school with the principal. Although it was hard to juggle construction, interviewing key people and looking after Oscar Poscar (as Norbu liked to call him), I wanted him to see the village for himself and understand how children can grow up in very different circumstances.

After landing at Paro, we spent time buying mattresses, bedding, books, buckets, a tin bath and other provisions. We loaded them into a big truck with an open back which Oscar was convinced would be OK for him to sit in on the journey. He climbed up to pose like a model on top of the piled mattresses before I broke the spell and he came down to sandwich himself between me and extra luggage on the back seat. Norbu drove and Rinzin helped with everything else.

We rattled along the bumpy 'road' from Gedu to Meritsemo and, after what Oscar was keen to point out was Such A Long Journey, we arrived at the village. We drove up the short incline to park by the small lhakang.

We were greeted by this same village lama and the young monks once again. We started to unpack the provisions from the truck. I looked round for Oscar and saw he was already gone, heading straight for the village school where we had arranged for him to take part in some of the lessons and get to know the children. Norbu ran after him, catching him up on the green path close by the school. Oscar was as keen to get to know Bhutan as I was!

The village reminded me of the *Asterix and Obelix* comic books my brother had so loved as a child, with a rural village of invincible Gauls. This Bhutanese village was also set in a horseshoe shape, set lower down from the lhakang with its buildings curling around the central school playing field. The houses were traditional in style, made of wood and straw and between them stray dogs were wandering around, their noses to the ground. In the books, the key characters, besides

Asterix and Obelix, were the chieftain, the musician and the wizard-druid. With Meritsemo so reminiscent of these childhood tales, I half expected one of them to pop up from behind a bushy gate. Along the path to the school buildings we did go past a shaggy-haired goat with eyes which seemed to look outwards from the sides of his head rather like a fish. There were numerous dogs, hens and butterflies. The families in the village were mostly farmers producing food to eat and also oranges and cardamom to sell to the nearby Indian market. Many of the adults were equipped with basic knives or machetes for cutting through foliage on the way to their fields. Often they were barefooted with conical straw hats set squarely on their heads like spires, designed to encourage the rain to drain down and away. They were a serious, hard-working people, up in the early hours and back tired and muddy late in the day. The school provided an essential service in the village both in terms of education and in keeping the children safe and occupied while their parents were off in the fields. In the daytime the village was deserted besides the children, a few hobbly old men and wandering animals.

Norbu told me later that the younger children had screamed in fear at the first sight of Oscar with his pale skin and the curly bright red hair of his Scottish heritage. It didn't seem to worry Oscar though and he soon had a little gang following him round and pushing him as high as possible on the home-built wooden swing. The latter creaked like an old barge every time it swung up and down – health and safety would be having kittens.

My suspicion that we were in the Bhutanese equivalent of *Asterix and Obelix* was confirmed when Oscar tugged at my arm later, saying, 'Look, Mummy, look – it's a wild boar.' And so it was, snuffling around on the edge of the village with its coarse hair visible on its back. Soon after, on the other side of the track, a young brown calf came running by, followed by a rope, followed by a young boy holding the end of the rope.

Oscar spent hours on the swing – being pushed by half the school, it seemed. I walked down to see them all and heard him calling out, 'Peeee, peeee.' Oscar, in line with most young children, likes a reference to bodily functions.

'Oh, Oscar, come on. Not that,' I said.

'No, Mummy, it's Dzongkha. I'm speaking Dzongkha. "Peeee" means "push" in Dzongkha.'

While he worked on these highlights of cultural integration, I spent much of my time with the principal of the primary school. I listened as he explained more about the reality of village life and how our fundraising could be of practical help to them. He wanted me to meet a few of the children who were living in the toughest of conditions, some who only had one parent still living. He also guided me through his vision for improving the quality of school life. I had thought it would all be about school books and pencils but, in fact, what he really wanted was a grass strimmer so the children would no longer have to cut the school ground's grass with knives. The day the grass strimmer arrived was a big day for everyone in the village.

With the help of Rinzin – who was increasingly showing himself to be a committed right-hand man – we took photos, discussed building plans and finalised future aims. Rinzin continued to take his role as host of his country very seriously. It was with Norbu that all the playful leg-pulling happened.

Oscar and I loved our days in the village. We didn't have a bath. We ate endless rice and heard lots of cocks crowing at dawn. We camped on makeshift beds in one of the teacher's houses and heard farmers outside the door chopping wood and bundling things up to carry on their backs early in the morning.

Village life was tough and in no way the endless sunshine of a comic book. Even so, to be part of it was truly wonderful and we were both sad to leave. Filled with the realisation of how great the village's need was and of the friendships we were making, we travelled back home to England.

I was surprised at the direction things were heading in. Something was growing strong in me, like the lean stem of the lotus leaving the mud and travelling upwards towards the light on the water's surface. On that surface a flower was opening and when it showed itself it seemed miraculous. Growing in the centre of this flower was set a clear determination to help others. I had thought that I could do very little but with students and friends it was possible to do more than I had ever imagined.

In my bedroom still, I can see the face of my golden Buddha lying on his side, smiling at me as I go about my life. I am surprised by the person I am now but perhaps he saw it all along.

After this second trip to the village I decided to have one of my big-picture chats with Brent over the phone. He had now moved back to New Zealand to run a hotel there but we were still often in touch and it was great to have someone to talk to who knows Bhutan so well.

'There's a lot to do and I do feel tired,' I had to admit. 'Oscar's been a handful again.'

'Well, you know you always do this – you're getting carried away,' Brent said. 'Just stop now. You've built the toilets and helped the school. Remember you're supposed to be a nun. You're supposed to be concentrating on your practice. You have ngongdro to finish [I was still completing stage three of ngondro at that point] and then there will be many other things to learn after that.'

'Yes, you're probably right,' I could hear myself say with a slight sigh. 'I *am* still practising though; every day. Some days not so much, but still every day.' I didn't say that I also wanted other people to benefit from my ordination and my practice – and that surely this work was a good way to do just that.

'If you carry on and register as a full-blown charity, you know you're going to be right back where you started– with a big corporate job and no time,' Brent continued.

'Hmm.'

'You'll just have built yourself a *massive* unpaid job,' Brent re-emphasised.

'Hmmm. You are probably right.' Even I could hear that I didn't sound totally convinced but Brent was right. It was bonkers. So much for simplifying my life. I was being a mum, training as a nun, learning Tibetan, teaching yoga and meditation, *and* contemplating running an international charity. The latter would require me to fork out loads of my own money to travel back and forth to obscure locations where I got monumental collections of flea bites which caused me to wrestle with my sleeping bag at night as I reached down to itch my swelling ankles.

But what else could I do? I felt I had a unique chance to help Bhutan, knowing it as well as I did by this stage. As long as I could afford it I could do my best to inspire people in Britain to help, and, then, in Bhutan, in my robes, I could help Bhutanese families. I was still a foreigner but I *was* a foreigner in robes. Two bookends were in place to make something wonderful possible.

It was strange to be engaging with a corporate-type activity with no hair and red robes, but it was a way of bringing all the skills and experiences I had accumulated and coming up with something truly helpful to others.

In early 2016, having made more progress on the ground in Bhutan, Adrienne and I decided to turn the fundraising initiative into a fully registered charity. We aimed to run the charity without spending money on employing staff while fulfilling the formal needs of being a registered charity. Luckily one of my newer yoga students, Sue, said she would like to help as a trustee, so this meant we had enough people to fill in all the necessary forms. Another student, Jane, offered to be the accountant and Simon was happy to continue running the website for free. Without this support, I could not have done it.

As a formal charity we needed a proper structure of trustees and a clear strategy for our work. I had to become the chief executive officer, an unusual title for someone with a shaved head and Tibetan prayer books. Ironic really – in my old life to be a CEO would have been a big achievement but it does fill me with slight embarrassment to carry a title which seems so incongruous with my clothing. Still I guess all my notions of what is possible were beginning to fade. If I could be active helping people in the world and deeply quiet in prayer, why not do it all?

But I had to wonder – where would this lead to next?

CHAPTER 28

UGYEN LA

An essential part of the confidence I had in being able to successfully achieve our projects in Bhutan had come from the arrival of a new person in my life. In late summer 2015, Rinzin, who had been helping with the initial work in Meritsemo, was offered a scholarship to study in the USA. It was a bit of a personal blow to hear this news although it was a great chance for him. It was essential to have someone dedicated on the ground if our work was to run smoothly.

Rinzin said a friend of his, Ugyen (pronounced *Oogen*), was really interested in getting involved. I told him I was very happy to meet him when I was next in Bhutan but I couldn't help but wonder whether his suggestion could be an act of politeness on his part as he did not want to let me down by leaving for America.

Before my next visit to Bhutan in October 2015, Ugyen messaged me to say he would like to meet. I replied, 'OK, I'm very busy but I have half an hour on Tuesday first thing.' It may have sounded abrupt but by this stage my short visits to Bhutan were packed with things to remember and provisions to buy for people. I had arrived in Paro happy as ever to be back in Bhutan and with a real sense of purpose now.

I had travelled on to Thimphu the morning after arriving to collect provisions before starting the long drive down to Meritsemo the day after. I would be researching our next project, probably a playground or school land drainage improvements, and more talks with Sonam, the school principal.

Up early and packed, I waited in the lobby of the basic hotel I had stayed at in Thimphu that morning. The lobby had wicker chairs not often seen in Bhutan and which reminded me of what you might see in a 1970s Surrey sun lounge. In walked a well-set, serious-looking Bhutanese man in a well-cared-for gho. I knew already that he was only 26 but his manner seemed to be that of a far more mature person. We sat down and he told me of how he really wished to do work which would help his country and its people. His sincerity and unselfishness were so great I thought he might be pulling my leg. I was amazed.

'Right,' I said. 'Now where are you living, la?'

'In Thimphu, Ani la.'

'How far from where we are now, la?' I enquired.

'Ten minutes in a taxi.'

'OK, well, we're leaving for Meritsemo in 25 minutes so if you really want to help us in our work, why don't you go home, pack a bag and come with us on this trip? We'll probably be gone around 4 days.'

I threw down the gauntlet! It was the closest I'd come in a long time to reclaiming my corporate-world brain. The speed of the decision was driven by the commitment to make this charity a real success.

Ugyen looked a little stunned. Extreme spontaneity was not the largest part of his DNA but, after a short moment, he said yes. I was pleased.

Norbu was driving again, and a new guide, Jigme, was helping with trip details. They finished squeezing sleeping bags, blankets, pillows, children's toys, our tents, biscuits and two big flasks of hot tea into the four-by-four.

Ugyen returned to the hotel with his bag and sleeping bag. Somehow we managed to fit in all four of us plus what looked like half a home store and we set off for the village.

Along the way we all got to know Ugyen a little. He was a serious chap. Unlike Norbu, who I chuckled away with and who let everything fall lightly off his shoulders – road blocks, fog, leeches – Ugyen had a liking for focused action which was just as well, because it turned out to be a seminal trip.

As we approached the village an enormous rainbow shone across the sky; a full bow of light connecting one side of the valley to the other. It had to be a good sign. We all jumped out of the car to take a photo of the Opening Your Heart to Bhutan team under the rainbow.

It was on this visit that I met Nakum (pronounced *Nar-Cum*). It was another name to get familiar with in my mouth. The school principal had mentioned to me that there was a girl I should see who had a problem walking, although no one really knew why. She received some small monetary help from the government but I had the impression things were still difficult. This was all I knew and that her house was off in 'that' direction further back from the principal's house.

Ugyen and I walked along a narrow, hard mud track between single-storey wooden houses, one at a particularly precarious angle. Joined by three puppies and two schoolboys, a few moments later we found ourselves walking up some grey wooden steps. At the top, on an open wooden porch a girl, who had to be Nakum, was sitting with her legs folded back behind her. Her head was on one side and her hair was long around a solemn face. Sitting there she looked a little like a beached mermaid. There were two low wooden blocks beside her and on each of them sat a cat. Not lying but sitting as if sentries at their posts on duty, their tails curling into their feet with ease... Their charge was this beautiful girl with a gentle face.

She sort of shuffled over into the main room of the house somehow using her knees and hands. Inside I sat with her on a small, red, flowered rug of the type typically used for a guest in a Bhutanese house. Nakum's mother, father and a couple of neighbours joined us and I was offered milky tea.

With Ugyen's help we slowly discovered her story. Nakum was 19 years old and, we learnt, had never walked. No one seemed quite sure why she was as she was. She went to hospital a while back but no one seemed quite sure of what her condition was or how to deal with it.

I had a strong feeling that there might be something we could do – after all, I did not see people sitting around like this in England. I checked with Nakum if it would be OK to check her lower legs and feet. They were warm and she confirmed she could feel my touch. I am no doctor but I felt that surely things could be better than this for Nakum, that perhaps she could even learn to walk. She had not had the chance to go to school and we were told she spent her days sitting in the house and on the porch. Her sadness was palpable; it hung about her.

Meeting Nakum was a powerful thing. Perhaps I was remembering Kathmandu, perhaps the man in Jakarta slumped against the wall, but perhaps it was something else. Perhaps I just wanted to help more than I had ever realised.

With the help of many people, particularly of a doctor called Dr Lotay in Bhutan, we were advised that Nakum had mild cerebral palsy but could, with some effort, have the chance of walking. It seemed too good a chance to turn down and Nakum was very keen to try.

Dr Lotay arranged for her to be transported the six hours north to Thimpu hospital. Here she had a full assessment of her situation.

Back in England, I waited to hear the news. Ugyen messaged me: *It's great news, Ani la, the doctors think in time she will definitely walk. I have seen her now in the hospital and she is doing great. She is doing her exercises and she is so happy, la.*

Ugyen sent me a photo of Nakum sitting on a hospital bed in pink-and-white pyjamas looking like the happiest person in the world – even though she still couldn't walk.

I couldn't wait to see her again.

Oscar was spending Christmas with Mark in 2015 so I was able to get back over to see Nakum as well as finalise our arrangements for building a playground for the school in Meritsemo. It was absolutely freezing arriving in Bhutan that December. I had forgotten the need to sleep in all your clothes – the grey English drizzle-dribble I had left behind seemed very benign in comparison. Highly wrapped up, I travelled from Paro to Thimpu. First stop: Nakum!

She was practising her walking in the second-floor hospital corridor when we arrived. I could see her arms working hard on the walking frame as she determinedly trained her legs beneath her to walk. Her body was slightly bent over with the effort. It was so wonderful to see her. She happily turned a corner and we followed her in to sit beside her on her hospital bed. I could already see the sadness, which had so weighed around her at our first meeting, had gone. Here was a young girl smiling, her beautiful face come alive. With the help of Ugyen we were able to talk, sitting together on the hospital bed.

'Can you ask her, Ugyen, how is she? Is she happy and not missing her family too much?' I was anxious on this point. I wanted to make sure the long distance and new environment were not too much for someone who had spent the largest part of her life in a small area of rural Bhutan.

They talked away and I waited.

'Ani la, she says she is so happy to be here and it's so interesting to see all these people. She had not realised she was not the only one like this. Here she has even seen people worse than her. She says that is giving her courage and determination. She really wants to walk, la.'

It had not occurred to me that Nakum might have thought she was the only one struggling in this way. I saw that her happiness was coming from finally feeling part of something, of fitting in at last. I gave her a big sideways hug on the bed and told her we would do all we could to help her.

I don't want to give you the impression that I am currently dashing round Bhutan looking under every nook and cranny for more Nakums. I think this was a special time and I feel very lucky to have found her. It just all came together again with that sense of certainty which seems to have become my best friend.

However, something very important came out of this meeting and that was Nakum leading us to discover a Bhutanese charity called Drak-tsho (pronounced *Drak So*). Although the name of the charity may be hard to pronounce, their work is amazing. They provide life skills and vocational training to children and young adults with special needs such as Nakum. In their schools these children can get an education, make friends and have the chance to develop a meaningful life and a sense of independence. Dr Lotay suggested that one of the charity's two schools was the perfect next step for her.

After her stay at Thimpu hospital, Nakum joined the boarding school of Drak-tsho in the east of Bhutan. This school seemed far away from her home village but Ugyen assured me it was an incredible opportunity and the doctors and Nakum herself were all keen to seize it. Attending the day school in Thimphu would be trickier as she would need an appropriate place to live in the city and this might not be easy to find with her family elsewhere.

Ugyen accompanied Nakum on the long bus journey from Thimpu to Trashigang in February 2016. In total it was six days there and back, including a stay over in Bumthang, waiting for a forest fire to die down, and numerous twists and turns in the buses fondly known as 'vomit comets' by the Bhutanese. Ugyen took his wife, Dechen, with him to help as Nakum was still using a frame to assist her walking. It was a demonstration of his dedication to the cause.

I wanted to see Nakum as soon as possible after she settled into her new home because I felt very responsible for her, having initiated this change in her life. In March 2016 I made my first trip into the eastern part of Bhutan with the express purpose of visiting her and seeing for myself the boarding school of Drak-tsho in the East. This was the sister school to its day school in Thimpu. Both had about 65 students in them.

Rather than face the long overland journey across Bhutan, I flew from Delhi to Guwahati in India then headed straight into eastern Bhutan. We were reunited on the Bhutanese/Indian border: Norbu, Ugyen, Jigme and me. Ugyen had arrived a couple of days earlier to oversee the delivery of a truckload of mattresses and bedding that our charity had donated to Drak-tsho then returned to the border to pick me up and tell me all the news.

Eastern Bhutan made western Bhutan seem like it was on speed. Everyone had said I would see the 'real Bhutan' by going east – well, in that case the real Bhutan is very quiet.

On the way up to the school, over a good 170 km of windy roads, we stopped off at various points and encountered little traffic. At the halfway point we took a twisting narrow road left, travelling on to visit Jigme's home village. He hadn't been able to get back to see his parents for a couple of years so this was a big deal and, to celebrate, as we sat on the floor of his aunt's wooden house, out came the vat of strong home-brewed liquor. Jigme became redder in the face and his eyes shone; joy or alcohol, I was not sure. Even I felt I became more animated despite not drinking – I think the fumes seeped into me.

Waking the next morning on a mattress in the family's shrine room, the air was rich with the sounds of cockerels and the smell of cow dung. We were again encountering people living mostly through subsistence farming which doesn't sound too tough in a geography lesson but looked relentless from what I could see. In layout and feel the village was what the Bhutanese might call a 'cousin-brother' to what we had seen in Meritsemo. Not a blood relation but definitely sharing similar features.

Norbu twisted his hands as if he were a magician turning cups up and down before me. 'Ani la, Bhutan – it's like this.'

'Yes, yes, I know, Norbu. What do you think I am, a foreigner?' I replied, laughing.

He shrugged and laughed back. 'Hard to say, la.'

It is from this kind of rural village that some children get the chance to join the Drak-tsho school near Trashigang. Here the children and young adults who attend as boarders return to their home villages during holidays. Some come from many hours' drive away as such facilities remain rare in Bhutan so far.

The school was still in the midst of construction. Perhaps a little less completed than I had imagined before embarking on the trip. This trip was focused on getting to know the school children and going through the practical details of how the school was managing and what they still needed. It was quickly obvious there was much to do so, while it was so inspiring to meet the children, the practical needs did feel a little daunting. But that was just how it was. *No matter*, I kept telling myself. *Concentrate on helping, Emma.*

Don't panic. Just focus on doing your best.

It can be a solitary occupation being a nun and these internal pep talks really help me.

Strangely, it's now more than ever that I am grateful for the analytical background I acquired in the corporate world. It gives me confidence to ask the necessary questions about the ideas and figures until I've got the full picture of any potential project. A nun asking detailed questions about drainage, soil types and the potential lifespan of zinc sheeting on roofs might seem incongruous but I have to investigate everything thoroughly. Then, back home, I can speak to others with a realistic understanding of the needs, costs and outcome of our work in Bhutan.

It was all worth it in the end. The accounting books laid out years ago on a table in New York, the constant questions to company bosses living in Asia, the general base level of determination to achieve the job in hand. The time and energy spent back then were finally allowing me to achieve something genuinely meaningful.

This visit to the school proved that Nakum was already a changed person. She was newly confident and wore a scarf round her neck at a rather jaunty angle. She had made two good girl friends who were both scouts – something the Bhutanese take very seriously. These friends explained that scouts take a vow to serve others and they were clearly choosing to enact this vow in taking care of Nakum and in helping her become part of their school. I was so pleased to see this. I had had a niggling worry that somehow she might feel isolated again in her new home at the school. To know this was not the case was a huge relief.

Next I officially handed out the bedding and new school uniforms that Ugyen had brought up in the truck a couple of days before. The students helped open up the huge bundles containing pillows, sheets and pillowcases and they stacked up the mattresses in large piles. I had felt a little embarrassed at the idea of handing out things to each individual student but the principal was adamant that the students would like this method best. In fact, it was a lovely occasion, if with slight Father Christmas overtones, and it gave me a chance to make sure I said hello and shook hands with or hugged every student. In all the effort to raise the funds for the bedding I must have forgotten the joy that comes from giving. It was good the school made me remember it again.

After everything had been given out, the principal said the students had prepared some dances to show me. On the wide concrete terrace, with the mountains of the Low Himalayas behind them, nine of the older students arranged themselves into three lines of three. The other students stood or sat around the edges in order to watch.

I was given a chair to sit on in front of the dancers. A big loudspeaker was brought out from somewhere and placed behind me in the doorway. Attached to the end of it, along a thin wire, was a small phone, propped up against the wall. The Bhutanese music began, sweet and rhythmic, and the dancers moved in perfect time, their hands elegant and expressive as they rotated them at shoulder height. I was entranced and impressed by their impeccable coordination but I couldn't quite ignore the ghastly crackling which was coming from the speaker. The equipment was much less competent than the dancers.

The principal rushed over, apologising and fiddling with the phone all at once; keen to put my ears out of their misery. He stopped the music. The dancers followed suit, surprised and disappointed.

'Oh, what a shame,' I said, joining in with the general droop of dismay. 'Is there anything else we can use maybe?' I asked, looking round as if some Sony executive might happen to be passing by with a spare amplifier.

'No, la,' came the Principal's answer. 'They don't usually use music.'

'Sorry?' I was a little confused.

'Well, they are all deaf, la. They don't hear the music.'

I paused, taken aback by Bhutan once again.

'They just do it all with counting, la,' he explained.

The penny dropped: that crackling music had only been for my benefit. It had not disturbed or indeed helped the dancers in the slightest.

'OK, I see,' I said. 'So let's continue then. Please ask them to start again, la. I don't need the music either.'

A few hand gestures were exchanged between the Principal and the dancers and we were back on again. The dancers were happily back in their lines, shaped against the blue haze of the mountains.

Soundless in the air, they began to dance.

It was spine-chilling.

'Incredible, right, la?' Ugyen whispered into my right ear.

'Incredible,' I agreed, stifling a sniffle with a pinch of my nose.

So far Ugyen has not let a tear fall on our visits whereas I find the sight of people trying their hardest in the face of such difficulty hard not to have a weep over. I straightened myself up and clapped with vigour as the dancing ended.

After milk tea and final chats, we left them all, me waving furiously out of the side window at the students crowding to say goodbye. Friends, hey – you never know where you're going to find them.

It started to rain as we drove down a road of loose sand, holes and moveable mud. By the time we had reached the bottom of the hill, another wonderful bright rainbow broke out like a song in the sky. We all jumped out and took our second team photo under the rainbow.

I didn't need any further confirmation that I was on the right track.

Working with Ugyen has become one of my absolute highlights of Bhutan. To see him so inspired by the charity projects we organise and the great care he takes with them has been a total joy. I keep expecting him to tell me he wants to jack it all in and concentrate on something more lucrative but so far I've been lucky. Spearheading the charity in the UK is a huge commitment and to have Ugyen on the ground in Bhutan has made all the difference. I owe him a huge debt of gratitude and hope we will always be friends.

Because of him and many other people, we have managed to help many children already and I remain determined to do what I can for the country I love so much.

Upon my return I was searching for ideas on how to inspire more people to assist us when one of my longest standing students, Michelle, offered her suggestion after a yoga class: 'Emma, I think you should write a book – write your story. I would buy it. That might really help your efforts in Bhutan.'

I thought about it but I had some reservations. I was only a little ani, still doing my preliminary practices and, anyway, surely this would be an act of ego?

I decided to ask Lama for his advice. 'Lama la, someone has suggested I write a book to help the fundraising for Bhutan but I'm worried it will seem like ego, talking about myself as if I'm someone important. What do you think?'

'It's good. Inspire others. Do it,' was his precise reply.

So, Lama la, here it is.

THE BEE THAT FLEW OUT
OF THE JAR

If you are wondering what the difference is between being a Buddhist and being a kind person, then I am pleased. This is the point. The robes help, the shaven head helps, renouncing desire helps, but Buddhism has taught me what I wanted to learn: how to be a kinder person. It's Kindhism, really, and so much else naturally follows on from that.

Perhaps, in the future, I *will* have the chance to go into a longer period of retreat under the guidance of my Lama in Bhutan. As I learn more about other forms of spiritual paths I notice many traditions place importance on retreat. It is definitely not an idea exclusive to Buddhism.

But when I discuss solitary retreats with people I realise it could sound like a crazy thing to do; to choose to experience physical confinement, removal from family and friends, being without TV or home comforts – and to deliberately volunteer for that! I wonder too. *I* also think it's hard to understand why someone would choose a retreat. The most important question for me is: what on earth could be the benefit of a retreat within the context of my wish to help others? This is what I ask myself, along with the usual questions of 'how will

I go to the loo?', 'how will I get food?' and 'what will I do if I get ill?' I won't hazard at guesses – I hope I will experience it. I can see and understand from my Lama that it is of great help, but he won't really articulate exactly how (no shortcuts here!).

I would like the chance to find out for myself. I am not afraid of going crazy on retreat or that I would be bored. But I'm concerned that a long period away from Oscar would be tough on him. I will only fulfil this dream if he's ready to stand easily on his own two feet. So I may not be retreating before the age of eighty.

Until then I will do all I can to remember the powerful practice of ahimsa, of kindness in everyday life. I hope our work with Opening Your Heart to Bhutan is only just beginning and that we will be able to do so much more that, by the time I can retreat, I'll be so exhausted that I'll happily flop into a cave in the Himalayas!

If I do go into retreat then perhaps, on my return, I will be able to explain more clearly what the purpose of it was; how it might be of help to me and others. Maybe it could even be the subject of another book, but perhaps it would be too hard to put such an experience into words. As Lama would say, 'How can you describe to someone the taste of honey?'

TEACHINGS FOR LIVING EVERY DAY

Here are some of the key things my Lama has told me which I try to remember to remember. I have summarised their potential benefits and I hope they are of use to you too.

Don't concentrate on what everyone else is doing.

Constantly looking at others, coming up with opinions on them, judging and repeating these judgements to yourself in your own mind is not the route to happiness.

Understand this habit creates suffering.

Concentrate on your own mind and on knowing your own mind. Don't attach to others or to methods always look at your own mind.

Develop awareness of your own mind at all times.

Ask yourself, 'Why are you doing your practice, if not to help others?'

The lens through which Lama encourages me to look at things is the question of whether or not what you are doing or saying or thinking is of help to other beings.

Understand the roots of happiness.

Is it bring you peaceful?

This was an early teaching to assist me in sorting helpful activities and words from unhelpful ones. It's a very useful, daily selection device. Ask yourself it. The strange sentence structure, straight from the mouth of my Lama, helps me remember it always with a smile.

Stop what is not helpful.

You must control the negative poisons of your mind, like a man carrying a pot of boiling oil on his head.

This was an interesting one for me as I had often heard that meditation was just a question of gently, and without attachment, watching thoughts come and go, so I was surprised at the use of the word 'control'. The Buddhist emphasis is on the practice of 'refraining' from checking the negative habits of the mind. Until one can practise positive action, speech and thought, the default setting is to refrain from anything negative. Learning this refraining is a close relation to learning 'control'. Its roots lie in ahimsa, non-harming.

Develop disciplined attention.

Fine to come on Tuesday morning, fine to come on Tuesday afternoon.

A teaching on the flexibility of the mind. It's a good one to deliberately practise, by finding happiness in letting things happen as they happen rather than unhappiness when they don't happen precisely according to your timetable. This is an easy one to forget in the West.

Develop ease of mind.

When teachings come to you like water, you must be as an upward-turned glass. If your glass is turned down, there is no chance the teachings will go in.

Teachings can come from anywhere, especially if your mind is open, as described here.

Cultivate an open attitude of mind at all times.

Look at any situation carefully. You must see the circumstances very clearly.

Lama's response to situations is very different from a 'they're the baddie, you're the goodie' type of thinking. It's an easy trap to fall into, especially in speech, but I try my best to avoid it. I aim to widen out my mind to see more than just simple black and white factors and this usually helps.

Use your human intelligence.

If it was easy, everyone would do it.

Lama says this when I have a lot to do and begin to feel weary.

Develop stamina and don't give up!

In addition to recalling these concentrated teachings, I find praying very useful. I have a wide definition of what 'praying' is, which is probably quite close to what many refer to as a state of 'mindfulness'.

To me, praying means bringing my mind into a state of awareness and directing it towards positive goals. Prayers can also be a call for guidance, whether you wish to see that guide as 'inside' or 'outside'. It's easy to get lost without a guide, without something to steer you to safety. As Buddhists we call this guide our 'Buddha nature'.

There are so many Buddhist prayers. I find this one particularly helpful. It is short and powerful. This is the prayer as it is shown in my preliminary texts in its three forms: the Tibetan script, the phonetic pronunciation of the Tibetan and the English translation.

The prayer asks that, even knowing there is suffering, we remain stable with our understanding and have the opportunity to clear away all these circles of suffering. These circles are often referred to by the Sanskrit term samsara where, like a bee trapped in a glass jar and unable to see the way out, the human mind can go round and round and not have the chance to see the origin of their suffering and do something about it. It seems that human life inevitably faces difficulty through being born into samsara and yet this prayer says that if we can develop kindness, even in the face of difficulty, we have the chance to wake up and find that our minds are, in fact, calm and clear.

ཟག་ལུས་འདི་དང་མ་འབྲལ་བར་དུ་ཡང་།

Zagluedee tang ma del bar du yang

Up until I abandon this body of mine,

འཁོར་བའི་སྡུག་བསྔལ་ཚོགས་ཀྱིས་མི་འཚེ་ཞིང་།

Khorwai du ngeltshokmitsheyzhing

**May I not be disturbed by the
total misery of samsara,**

མཐུན་རྐྱེན་མ་ལུས་ཕུན་སུམ་ཚོགས་པ་དང་།

Thuen ken ma luephuesoomtshok pa tang

May I have all the conditions for living a perfect life and

འགྲོ་བའི་སྡུག་བསྔལ་སེལ་བའི་མཐུ་ལྡན་ཤོག།

Drowai du ngel se waithu den shok.

Have the power to clear away the sufferings of the samsara.

THE OPENING YOUR HEART TO BHUTAN CHARITY

Opening Your Heart to Bhutan is a fully registered UK charity (number 1165794), set up by Emma Slade. Proceeds from this book will go towards the work of this charity in Bhutan.

The charity works to achieve tangible and long-lasting improvements in the quality of life of children in Bhutan, particularly those in rural areas and/or with additional special needs.

Details of its work to date and ongoing projects can be found at **www.openingyourhearttobhutan.com** and at its Facebook page. Previous achievements include building a fully equipped school playground in rural Bhutan, building a hostel for 30 disabled girls in eastern Bhutan and providing school vehicles to enable children to access both schools and hospitals.

Emma will try her best to respond personally to any queries about its work through the charity email address **beingkindinbhutan@gmail.com** and is always delighted to give talks and make new friends in her goal of developing the work of the charity far and wide to the benefit of all.

If you are inspired to help the charity in any way, do contact Emma or look on the website for details about donating funds or donations in kind such as skills, goods and good wishes.

Details of Emma's book-related activities can be found at **www.emmaslade.com**.

If you have enjoyed this book, we would love to see a photo of you reading the book, wherever you may be. Post it to Twitter or Facebook with the hashtag **#SetFree**.

ABOUT THE AUTHOR

Emma Slade is an ordained Buddhist nun, yoga and meditation teacher, and author. She is based in Whitstable, Kent, but spends several months per year in Bhutan where she set up and runs her charity, Opening Your Heart to Bhutan. Emma can be found on Facebook under Pema Deki and on Twitter @emmabhutan

Emma in London, 2005

Emma in Bhutan, 2012

BIG THANK YOUS

Marilyn
    Ngawang
Cora and Richard
    Michelle and Guy
Bridget
  Mia
    Adrienne
      Sue
        Pete
      Ima
   Lucy
Sandra
      Alexandra
   Mum
Toby
   Becky
    Graznya
  Oscar

THE HONEY BEES
  Julie
   Jo
   Joy
Donna and Karen

Rinzin
Ugyen
Norbu
Brent
Aum Sonam
Penden
The Yangphel Family

BHUTAN

I wish to thank Joanna Swainson for her courage in backing an unknown author and to all at Summersdale Publishers who have worked so hard to make this the best book it could be.

The kindness of all the people who have joined with me in helping children in Bhutan has been deeply moving to me. You have shown me that kindness can indeed grow like a lotus flower, emerging from the dark waters of a deep lake, and then, with your support, flourish into something amazing. Thank you all.

LAUREN JULIFF

HOW NOT TO TRAVEL THE WORLD

*Adventures of a
disaster-prone backpacker*

HOW NOT TO TRAVEL THE WORLD

Adventures of a Disaster-Prone Backpacker

Lauren Juliff

ISBN: 978-1-84953-727-8

£9.99

I had no life experience, zero common sense and had never eaten rice. I suffered from debilitating anxiety, was battling an eating disorder and had just had my heart broken. I hoped by leaving to travel the world I would be able to heal myself.

Instead, Lauren's travels were full of bad luck and near-death experiences. Over the space of a year, she was scammed and assaulted; lost teeth and swallowed a cockroach. She fell into leech-infested rice paddies, was caught up in a tsunami, had the brakes of her motorbike fail and experienced a very unhappy ending during a massage in Thailand. It was just as she was about to give up on travel when she stumbled across a handsome New Zealander with a love of challenges...

A SHORT RIDE
IN THE JUNGLE

THE HO CHI MINH TRAIL BY MOTORCYCLE

ANTONIA BOLINGBROKE-KENT

A SHORT RIDE IN THE JUNGLE

The Ho Chi Minh Trail by Motorcycle

Antonia Bolingbroke-Kent

ISBN: 978-1-84953-543-4

£9.99

'For the first time in my life I felt that death was a possibility; a stupid, pointless, lonely death on the aptly named Mondulkiri Death Highway.'

The Ho Chi Minh Trail is one of the greatest feats of military engineering in history. But since the end of the Vietnam War much of this vast transport network has been reclaimed by jungle, while remaining sections are littered with a deadly legacy of unexploded bombs. For Antonia, a veteran of ridiculous adventures in unfeasible vehicles, the chance to explore the Trail before it's lost forever was a personal challenge she couldn't ignore - yet it would sometimes be a terrifying journey.

Setting out from Hanoi on an ageing Honda Cub, she spent the next two months riding 2000 miles through the mountains and jungles of Vietnam, Laos and Cambodia. Battling inhospitable terrain and multiple breakdowns, her experiences ranged from the touching to the hilarious, meeting former American fighter pilots, tribal chiefs, illegal loggers and bomb disposal experts.

The story of her brave journey is thrilling and poignant: a unique insight into a little known face of Southeast Asia.

Have you enjoyed this book?
If so, why not write a review on your favourite website?

If you're interested in finding out more about our books,
find us on Facebook at **Summersdale Publishers** and
follow us on Twitter at **@Summersdale**.

Thanks very much for buying this Summersdale book.

www.summersdale.com